O IT! Scenarios of the Revolution

Stephan Shames

DO

Scenarios of

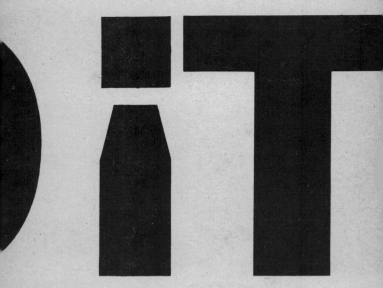

DiT

*the Revolution
by Jerry Rubin*

Introduction by Eldridge Cleaver

*Designed by Quentin Fiore
Yipped by Jim Retherford
Zapped by Nancy Kurshan*

Ballantine Books   New York

To Nancy, Dope, Color TV, and Violent Revolution!

JERRY RUBIN is the leader of 850 million Yippies.

In a previous life Jerry was a sports reporter and a straight college student. He dropped out, visited Cuba and moved to Berkeley where he became known as the P.T. Barnum of the revolution, organizing spectacular events such as marathon Vietnam Day marches, teach-ins, International Days of Protest.

Jerry lived for three years near the University of California working as an Outside Agitator to destroy the university. He ran for Mayor of Berkeley and came within one heart attack of winning in a four-man race.

Jerry moved to New York in October 1967 and became Project Director of the March on the Pentagon. He appeared before "witch-hunt" committees of Congress dressed as an American Revolutionary War soldier, a bare-chested, armed guerrilla and Santa Claus. With Abbie Hoffman, Jerry created the Yippies as a fusion between the hippies and the New Left, and helped mobilize the demonstrations during the Democratic National Convention in Chicago in August 1968.

The U.S. Government indicted Jerry and seven other revolutionaries for conspiracy to destroy the Democratic Convention, resulting in "The Conspiracy," perhaps the most important political trial in the history of the country.

Jerry wants to hear *your* reactions to this book. If you want to write him about that or anything else, write: Jerry Rubin, c/o Brandt & Brandt, 101 Park Avenue, New York, N.Y. 10017 (mailing address only).

READ THIS BOOK STONED!

Copyright © 1970 by Social Education Foundation
Library of Congress Catalog Card Number: 71-107258
All rights reserved.

Hardbound SBN 671-20535-8
Trade Paperbound SBN 671-20601-X

SBN 345-02038-3-125

This edition published by arrangement with
Simon & Schuster.

First Printing: October, 1970

Printed in the United States of America

BALLANTINE BOOKS, INC.
101 Fifth Avenue, New York, N.Y. 10003

An INTEXT Publisher

Contents

Child of Amerika 12

Elvis Presley Killed Ike Eisenhower 17

The Middle of the Beast 20

FSM: Shut the Motherfucker Down! 21

Become a 100-Foot-Tall Nonstudent 24

Troop Trains Coming Through Our Town, Tra-la, Tra-la 32

It's Gotta Be More Fun to Be In the Revolution Than Out of It 37

"A Movement That Isn't Willing to Risk Injuries, Even Deaths, Isn't for Shit" 39

Any Fool Can Run for Mayor 47

We Are All Human Be-ins· 54

HUAC Creates Subpoenas Envy and Meets Thomas Jefferson 57

Hollywood Casts the Peace Movement for the Battle of the Pentagon 66

How to Be a Yippie 81

Our Leaders Are Seven-Year-Olds 87

Don't Trust Anyone Over 40 89

Long Hair, Aunt Sadie, Is a Communist Plot 92

Keep Pot Illegal 98

Ho Chi Minh Is a Yippie Agent 102

Every Revolutionary Needs a Color TV 106

Fuck God 109

Ideology Is a Brain Disease 113

Money Is Shit—Burning Money, Looting and Shoplifting Can Get You High 117

I Agree With Your Tactics, I Don't Know About Your Goals 125

Revolution Is Theater-in-the-Streets 132

George Wallace Is Bobby Kennedy in Drag 144

Are the Kennedys Assassination-Prone? 149

Free the Prisoners and Jail the Judges 152

Sirhan Sirhan Is a Yippie 161

The Battle of Czechago 168

The Nomination and Election of Pigasus, the Pig, as President of the United States 176

My "Bodyguard" Turns Out to Be a Czechago Pig 181

How Amerikan Airlines, Richard Nixon, Spiro Agnew, Strom Thurmond, John Mitchell, Walter Cronkite, CBS, NBC, ABC, Uncle Ho and a Million Spirits Conspired to Burn Czechago Down 186

The Academy Award of Protest Acceptance Speech 191

Yippie-Panther Pipe Dream No. 2 195

HUAC Digs Che's Painted Tits But Bars Santa Claus 201

Burn Down the Schools 209

"Welcome Home, Jerry!" 216

People's Park Will Rise Again 224

It's Against the Law to Pee in the Streets 231

We Cannot Be Co-opted Because We Want Everything 235

We Are All Eldridge Cleaver 241

The Viet Kong Are Everywhere 246

Scenario for the Future/ Yippieland 253

I started writing an "Introduction" to this book by Jerry Rubin. I fucked with the "Introduction" for a few days, but couldn't get into it right. I was writing shit like this: "I first met Jerry Rubin . . ." Then a few positive things happened, among which I turned on. Then I started fucking with the "Introduction" again and suddenly realized that what was wrong, what was bugging me, was that I was trying to write an "INTRODUCTION" to Jerry's book. Fuck that shit. This is no "Introduction." I'm just glad for this chance to run some shit down, cut up some things, in the context of relating to Jerry. So right on.

The first chapter of Jerry's book is entitled "Child of Amerika." That's another one of Jerry's trips. It is impossible for him to be a child of Amerika—no matter how he spells it. Jerry is not an Indian. He is a descendant of the invaders. I am in favor of a Dictatorship by the Indians. It's their land. I don't care how few of them there may be left: if there is only one single Indian left, I am in favor of making him an absolute monarch, even if he is an idiot. The Indians have a right to that. I am not interested in any arguments to the contrary. All arguments have been thoroughly refuted by the heroic resistance against the European invaders put up by the Indians led by great leaders such as Tecumseh, Sitting Bull and Geronimo.

But Jerry is a child of something. He calls that Amerika. What the Indians really feel about that is not taken into consideration. O.K. Jerry is a child of the Amerika that does not take the Indians into consideration. We need language that condenses all this shit into phrases. Most of Amerika's history can be boiled down to one five-letter word: BLOOD. Jerry is the child of BLOOD.

What a child! Scornful of his elders who are too old even for the Fountain of Youth to help. Too old in their ways, too old in their values, too old in their pride, and too old in their avarice. And too old in their belief in the power of their world. Jerry wants to up the Age of Trust to 40 years old. I want to lower it to 20.

When I was nominated for President by the Peace and Freedom Party, Jerry Rubin was my choice for Vice. I had done a little soul searching. I asked myself, one night while I was lying awake thinking about what I could do for my country, if I were elected President, who would I want for Vice? Who is the man or woman I would want to succeed me if I became unable to carry out the duties of the Presidency? The answer came like a flash, like a bolt of lightning: Jerry. If everybody did exactly what Jerry suggests in this book—if everybody carried out Jerry's program—there would be immediate peace in the world. Amerika, in particular, would cease to bleed.

I do not believe that everybody is going to follow Jerry's program, which makes me sad, because that means we must think in terms of alternatives. But that is no big thing. I always think in terms of alternatives to all programs, suggestions, whispers, etc. There is something wrong with all programs. They can all be improved. I always try to support the best program I know about. After the program I support, I like Jerry's program best. So I support Jerry's program now, because we must keep an alternative near at hand, within easy reach. Humanity cannot afford to get locked into any program, but Humanity always functions on the basis of a program. A program of many scripts, each little group of actors following the script around which they are united.

I can unite with Jerry Rubin around a marijuana cigarette, around some good music, around being cool, around a profound contempt for pigs, and around the need for moving to change the world in which we live. I can unite with Jerry around hatred of pig judges, around hatred of capitalism,

7

around the total desire to smash what is now the social order in the United States of Amerika. Around the dream of building something new and free upon the ruins.

Although I do not relate to Santa Claus, it doesn't bother me that Jerry *appeared* (out of Amerika's nighmares!) at the HUAC Hearings dressed as Santa Claus. I was glad and it made me feel good when Jerry freaked those pigs out and blew their Hearing up their ass. Elijah Muhammad says that "the Devils try to steal a hearing." These pigs have to steal their hearings. They are totally dependent upon spies, agents, informers, whitemail, napes, and cop-outs for their information, because they themselves are out of it. The geeks against whom Jerry makes war, we make war, are culturally, intellectually, politically, economically, and emotionally incapable of getting close to the action. They need a base in the terrain of someone else's brain. They have many bases. Oppressed, exploited, and colonized people are colonized, oppressed and exploited on all levels. Intellectually, Politically, Economically, Emotionally, Sexually, and Spiritually we are oppressed, exploited, and colonized. Some of us work for the pigs. Some of us are pigs. Some of us kill pigs. All of us are fucked up. The oppressed are fucked up for not fighting decisively to end their own oppression, and the oppressors are fucked up for resisting the change. Jerry Rubin fights hard against the pigs and their world of blood.

Huey said that within a short time the Black Panther Party will have millions of members. Jerry said that the Kindergarten Children are a rising wave of Yippies. And judging from some Kindergarten Teachers whom I know personally, I say Jerry is right. I know Huey is right.

If Huey and Jerry are correct about the future, then it is easy to understand why rapacious pigs need all the Hearings they can get. It's easy to understand why a dirty motherfucking pig feels the oinkish need to tap telephones, to sneak up on you and take you by surprise, like a hunter. Just picture a lousy pig stealing a Hearing over a tapped phone. What the fuck is he into? Who the fuck does he think he is, with his big ears? Jerry makes us laugh at these pigs from their comic exposure, because he knows that once the people laugh at the king, laugh at their rulers, see them as a preposterous joke and fraud, the people will next rise up and kill pigs and destroy their power. A laughed-at pig is a dead pig, barbecued Yippie style. I can dig that, but I relate most heavily to pig barbecued on the Block. I would say that my favorite barbecued pig is what brothers and sisters call Willow Street Pig, or Chef Ahamed's Special Pig Roast.

What kind of ceremony are we going to stage to celebrate our triumph over the pigs? It won't be another Fourth of July! At least on the Kindergarten level, it may be a bad idea to stage the Inauguration of Pigasus and explain it to the little hip tots by saying, "Once upon a time, a class of exploiters and oppressors ruled our country and the people called them pigs. They called them pigs because . . ."

I, along with many other people, feel personally outraged by the game that the pigs have been running down. This gives me a chance to put forward an alternative interpretation of the Democratic National Convention held in Chicago in August 1968.

Most people are eager to say that the pigs flipped out, or that they finally showed their true colors. I disagree, I believe that what happened in Chicago is a direct result of conspiracies hatched by the Republican Party and those who supported Nixon for President, working hand in hand with the racist, right-wing John Birchers who control the Chicago Police Department just as they control the police departments in many important cities throughout the country. The Republicans knew that they had to move in a decisive manner or risk the Democrats' winning the election by a close margin. Nixon, having lost once on a cliff-hanger, was not taking any more chances. So someone dreamed up the greedy idea of shocking the American people into fear and hysteria and at the same time both wrecking the Democratic National Convention and firmly establishing in the minds of the American people the image of the Democrats as being responsible for the violence going down in Babylon. The situation was made to order for a pig setup. And it worked. There is a danger to the healthy development of the American Revolution in the fact that often revolutionaries are manipulated by the ruling class to appear as a bigger threat than they really are. This is done by right-wing elements who need an atmosphere of hysteria in which to work; otherwise they would never be able to attract the people to their desperate, hopeless strategies. By unleashing ferocious violence in Chicago, the right wing was able to shock the nation, panic the people, and give rise to a "kick the rascals out" sentiment that could not be blocked by that stupid fucker Hubert Humphrey. Now the whole thing is being blamed on the revolutionary forces. Nixon is safely in office.

On the night of October 27, 1967, in the wee wee hours of that darkness, guns blazed in the heart of Black Oakland, on Seventh and Willow streets. The quiet of the night was shattered by the minor thunder of the guns. Death stalking a circle around warring men, and the shadow of death was created by the blaze leaping from the barrel of a gun. A pig white lay dead, deep fried in the fat of his own bullshit. And another pig white lay there, similar to the dead one in every respect except that he did not die. This was a rare moment of death for the oppressor and triumph for the oppressed. This beautiful spark of glory on the streets in the dark in Babylon lights the way for Lil Bobby to find room in which to die a warrior's death, and light to show those who remain and fight on how to finish the job of offing the pigs.

"Prison, where is thy victory?" Minister of Defense Huey P. Newton has asked. Black people do not accept, and have firmly rejected, and are fighting against, racist oppression at home and imperialist aggression abroad. In prison, on the streets, in the courts, outside the country, the answer is one and the same: *Off the Pigs.* It is time for Amerika's children to start killing and dying for themselves, and stop exporting the revolution and the deaths that we must die.

Toward the end of December 1966, almost three years ago, I accompanied Beverly Axelrod to Stew Albert's pad in Berkeley. It was late afternoon. Jerry and Nancy, Stew, Joann, Jack Weinberg and perhaps others were present, but these I don't remember. I had been out of prison for barely a couple of weeks, and Beverly was introducing me to her friends. These were cats whose activities in the FSM and Vietnam Day Committee I had read about while in prison. I looked forward to the day when I'd be free and would have the chance to meet these cats and perhaps work with them.

This was our first meeting. We turned on and talked about the future. No one was quite sure of just how they would move. Yippie was as yet an uncoined word, and I had not yet encountered the Black Panther Party. We were in agreement, of course, on what basically had to be done, but it was clear that much had to be created before our dreams could be realized.

At that time, the black movement and the white movement were not speaking to each other. Stokeley Carmichael was the leader of SNCC, and was on his way up to the zenith of the authority of his rap. Now, as I write this, Stew Albert and his rib, Gumbo, are guests in my pad here in Alger. Jerry is on trial in Chicago along with the chairman of the Black Panther Party, Bobby Seale, and along with Tom Hayden, Dave Dellinger, Abbie Hoffman, Rennie Davis, Lee Weiner and John Froines. Thinking back to that evening in Stew's pad in Berkeley, I remember the huge poster of W. C. Fields on the ceiling, and the poster of Che on the wall—Che, with his farseeing eyes, staring fiercely and fearlessly into the revolutionary future and at the death which he surprised with his heroic welcome. None of us knew, that night, what the future would be, except that we all knew that we would be trying. And we have tried. And we will continue to try. And we will have successes that will surprise us. In this book, Jerry has detailed, in a very readable fashion, the essence of the efforts that he has made, and in doing so, he tells us much of what he knows about Amerika, things we all need to know.

The other night I talked to Jerry on the telephone— Alger to Babylon—and he almost bubbled right through the receiver the way he bubbles through this book . . . the way he bubbles through life. In publishing this book a child of Amerika goes on trial before Amerika. In reading it, Amerika will be surprised to learn that, in fact, Amerika is on trial before the child, before all its children. And for a verdict, the children are screaming for Amerika's death. Right on.

All Power To The People
Eldridge Cleaver

Alger, Algeria
November 4, 1969

1 : Child of Amerika

I am a child of Amerika.

If I'm ever sent to Death Row for my revolutionary "crimes," I'll order as my last meal: a hamburger, french fries and a Coke.

I dig big cities.

I love to read the sports pages and gossip columns, listen to the radio and watch color TV.

I dig department stores, huge supermarkets and airports. I feel secure (though not necessarily hungry) when I see Howard Johnson's on the expressway.

I groove on Hollywood movies—even bad ones.

I speak only one language—English.

I love rock 'n' roll.

I collected baseball players' cards when I was a kid and wanted to play second base for the Cincinnati Reds, my home team.

I got a car when I was sixteen after flunking my first driver's test and crying for a week waiting to take it a second time.

I went to the kind of high school where you had to pass a test to get *in*.

I graduated in the bottom half of the class.

My classmates voted me the "busiest" senior in the school.

I had short, short, short hair.

I dug *Catcher in the Rye*.

I didn't have pimples.

I became an ace young reporter for the Cincinnati *Post and Times-Star*. "Son," the managing editor said to me, "*someday you're going to be a helluva reporter, maybe the greatest reporter this city's ever seen.*"

I loved Adlai Stevenson.

My father drove a truck delivering bread and later became an organizer in the Bakery Drivers' Union. He dug Jimmy Hoffa (so do I). He died of heart failure at fifty-two.

My mother had a college degree and played the piano. She died of cancer at the age of fifty-one.

I took care of my brother, Gil, from the time he was thirteen.

I dodged the draft.

I went to Oberlin College for a year, graduated from the University of Cincinnati, spent 1½ years in Israel and started graduate school at Berkeley.

I dropped out.

I dropped out of the White Race and the Amerikan nation.

I dig being free.

I like getting high.

I don't own a suit or tie.

I live for the revolution.

I'm a yippie!

I am an orphan of Amerika.

16

2: *Elvis Presley Killed Ike Eisenhower*

The New Left sprang, a predestined pissed-off child, from Elvis' gyrating pelvis.

> *tell ya somethin' brother*
> *found a new place to dwell*
> *down on the end of Lonely Street*
> *it's Heartbreak Hotel.*

On the surface the world of the 1950's was all Eisenhower calm. A cover story of "I Like Ike" father-figure contentment.

Under the surface, silent people railed at the chains upon their souls. A latent drama of repression and discontent.

Amerika was trapped by her contradictions.

Dad looked at his house and car and manicured lawn, and he was proud. All of his material possessions justified his life.

He tried to teach his kids: he told us not to do anything that would lead us from the path of Success.

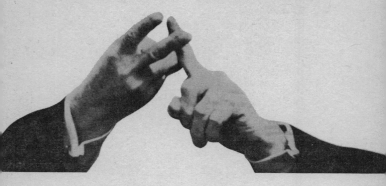

work *don't play*
study *don't loaf*
obey *don't ask questions*
fit in *don't stand out*
be sober *don't take drugs*
make money *don't make waves*

We were conditioned in self-denial:

We were taught that fucking was bad because it was immoral. Also in those pre-pill days a knocked-up chick stood in the way of Respectability and Success.

We were warned that masturbation caused insanity and pimples.

And we were confused. We didn't dig why we needed to work toward owning bigger houses? bigger cars? bigger manicured lawns?

We went crazy. We couldn't hold it back any more.

Elvis Presley ripped off Ike Eisenhower by turning our uptight young awakening bodies around. Hard animal rock energy beat/surged hot through us, the driving rhythm arousing repressed passions.

Music to free the spirit.

Music to bring us *together*.

Buddy Holly the Coasters, Bo Diddley, Chuck Berry, the Everly Brothers, Jerry Lee Lewis, Fats Domino, Little Richard, Ray Charles, Bill Haley and the Comets, Fabian, Bobby Darin, Frankie Avalon: they all gave us the life/beat and set us free.

Elvis told us to *let go!*

                    let go!
                      let go!
                        let go!
                        let go!
                       let go!
                      let go!
                     let go!
                    let go!
                   let go!
                 let go!
                let go!
               let go!
              let go!
             let go!

18

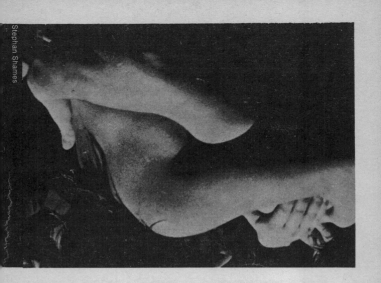

Stephan Shames

Affluent culture, by producing a car and car radio for every middle-class home, gave Elvis a base for recruiting.

While a car radio in the front seat rocked with "Turn Me Loose," young kids in the back seat were breaking loose. Many a night was spent on dark and lonely roads, balling to hard rock beat.

The back seat produced the sexual revolution, and the car radio was the medium for subversion.

Desperate parents used permission to drive the car as a power play in the home: "If you don't obey, you can't have the car Saturday night."

It was a cruel weapon, attacking our gonads and our means of getting together.

The back seat became the first battleground in the war between the generations.

Rock 'n' roll marked the beginning of the revolution.

19

3 : The Middle of the Beast

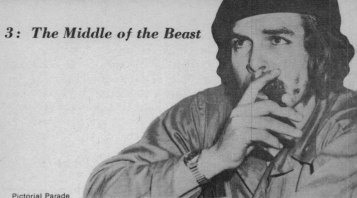

Pictorial Parade

Che stood before us in the Ministry of Labor auditorium. He was shorter than we expected, about 5 feet 10 inches tall. He wore an olive-green military uniform with a revolver at his hip. He embraced us with his intensity and joy.

We were 84 Amerikan students visiting Cuba illegally in 1964. We had to travel 14,000 miles, via Czechoslovakia, to reach Cuba, 90 miles off the Florida coast.

As Che rapped on for four hours, we fantasized taking up rifles. Growing beards. Going into the hills as guerrillas. Joining Che to create revolutions throughout Latin America. None of us looked forward to returning home to the political bullshit in the United States.

Then Che jolted us out of our dream of the Sierra Madre. He said to us:

You North Amerikans are very lucky. You live in the middle of the beast.

You are fighting the most important fight of all, in the center of the battle.

If I had my wish, I would go back with you to North Amerika to fight there.

I envy you.

4: FSM: Shut the Motherfucker Down!

It began with a 14-word edict issued by a Berkeley campus dean outlawing political tables and leafleting for the purpose of organizing demonstrations off the campus.

We were amazed. Surely it must be a problem of "communication." But every dean we talked to said: "I can't do anything about it. I'm not responsible. But you'll have to obey the rules."

And the president of the university, Clark Kerr? No one even knew what *he* looked like.

Then we learned the *inside story:* The previous year we used the campus to organize massive civil rights demonstrations against the hotel and auto industries in San Francisco. The very same racists who controlled the business world controlled the university too! And they were trying to protect their businesses by attacking us at our base, the university. They were the Regents.

The Regents were at their Country Clubs, and they would rather shit on a student than talk to him.

We put up civil rights tables in the middle of the campus.

We decided to deliberately break the new rules.

A police car pulled onto Sproul Plaza. Cops were leading one arrested activist into the car when somebody shouted, "Sit down!"

Within seconds the car was surrounded by a few hundred people. Within minutes our numbers grew to 2,000.

Inside the police car was Jack Weinberg, a prisoner of the pigs. But we surrounded the pigs, and they were our prisoners.

We demanded *his* release in exchange for *their* release. The cops would have to drive the car over our bodies to take our brother to jail.

UNIVERSITY OF CALIFORNIA

PROPERTY OF THE REGENTS OF
THE UNIVERSITY OF CALIFORNIA
PERMISSION TO ENTER OR PASS
OVER IS REVOCABLE AT ANY TIME

We climbed on top of the police car to rap about what was going down. For the next 10 hours into the night, 5,000 people packed into the Berkeley campus square for the greatest class we ever attended.

As we surrounded the car, we became conscious that we were a new community with the power and love to confront the old institutions.

Our strength was our willingness to die together, our unity.

We created our own spontaneous government. People formed communes to make sandwiches for those surrounding the car. Committees notified the media and contacted students across the country, and we created a negotiating team in case the university was interested.

Thirty-two hours later, we heard the grim roar of approaching Oakland motorcycle cops behind us. I took a deep breath. "Well, this is as good a place to die as any."

But as we prepared to meet the heavy club of the Man, the university suddenly dropped charges against our arrested brother and agreed to "negotiate."

The deans found themselves up against the wall for the first time in Amerika.

They didn't dig it.

Two months later, we learned a heavy bureaucrat trick: the fucking deans were using "negotiations" as a dodge to wear us out. Talk, talk, talk while the rules against political activity stood strong.

We got very pissed off.

Fuck this shit!

So one beautiful sunny noon, Joan Baez sang, Mario Savio orated and a thousand people walked into the administration building to shut the motherfucker down.

At 4 A.M. the governor, a liberal Democrat, ordered the Oakland cops to clear the building:

800 persons were arrested, the biggest single bust in Amerikan history.

The sight of cops on campus threw all the fence-sitters, including the professors, right into the arms of the extremists.

Students retaliated with a strike that crippled the university. We destroyed the university's moral authority.

The only authority left on campus was the Free Speech Movement. The Regents and deans had no power. Students could do anything we wanted.

Students became the biggest political force in the state with the university as our guerrilla stronghold.

We held power on campus because we were the majority there. But off-campus the politicians, courts and cops were hollering for our balls.

The war against Amerika
in the schools
and the streets
by white middle-class kids
thus commenced.

23

5: *Become a 100-Foot-Tall Nonstudent*

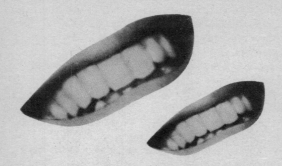

The Free Speech Movement invited young kids to come to Berkeley for the action. So thousands of refugees from New York and the Midwest flocked to live on the streets of Berkeley.

It was an easy life. The weather was warm and the seasons hardly changed, so you didn't need to buy winter clothing. You could always get by selling dope. Or you could hawk the *Barb* on the weekend and make enough money for the rest of the week. There were always guilty professors to panhandle. And some people started handicraft industries—sold jewelry, candles and other things they made—right on the Avenue.

Nobody starved in the streets of Berkeley.

A whole new culture burst forth just outside the biggest university in the history of the world. Telegraph Avenue was five blocks long lined with bookstores, outdoor cafes, poster shops and underground movie theaters.

Dig the straight student who came out of a Los Angeles suburb to get an education at Berkeley. Heading for his dormitory or apartment after a hard day at school, he passed down Telegraph Avenue: like walking through the revolution on the way home.

He would pass a record shop and catch a couple of lines of Dylan.

A middle-class suburban kid just like himself, except looking like a barefoot Jesus Christ, would walk up and ask him, "Any spare change?"

Gradually the thought entered the consciousness of the straight student:

"Here I am burdened by assignments, responsibilities, guilts, no time my own. And here are these hippies on the streets; they can do whatever they want to. They can get high all day. They can stay in the sun all day, while I have to spend my time in a stuffy classroom, listening to boring professors and taking exams that are making me a nervous wreck."

The university is a place for making it, a high-pressured rat race. Competition for grades, degrees, books, recommendations, getting into graduate school and getting a good job.

The academic world is a hierarchy, and everybody's always kissing the ass of the guy on top of him.

But all the students saw the living example of thousands of young kids who had given up on the straight world and who were free even though they hadn't reached retirement age. They were real students in the classical sense of education as self-growth. And since many of the hippies were ex-students, they had the zealous mission of reformed sinners.

Students started hanging around nonstudent tables, and forgetting to go to their classes.

As their hair lengthened, their interest in schoolwork shortened.

As they smoked more and more dope, they found their exams and research papers more and more absurd.

They started dropping out of school—in droves.

25

Al Copeland

The wildest teacher at the University of California was Stew Albert. Stew sat behind the table of the Vietnam Day Committee and attracted massive crowds because he was the first revolutionary anyone ever saw with flowing blond hair and devilish blue eyes. But soon as they looked, they got hooked by Stew into ferocious controversy about pot, Vietnam, God, the university, sex and Communism.

It must have outraged the university professors. They had to *force* people to attend *their* classes through threats —rewards and punishments.

But here was Stew, holding everyone's attention just because they dug rapping freely.

Stew was teaching under the sun, instead of in a stale classroom. But he had *no right* to teach. He hadn't gone through the Credentials Factory like everyone else. He was a dropout.

The university became a fortress surrounded by our foreign culture, longhaired, dopesmoking, barefooted freeks who were using state-owned university property as a playground. It threatened the integrity of the university. It freaked out the politicians of the state.

The politicians considered us *traitors*—and we were traitors using tax money to carry out our treason.

The conservative forces in the state pressured the university to clean up the *foreign scum*.

The university readily agreed, because it discovered the *vermin* corrupting from within as well as without.

The university began "Operation Pacification": separate the "people" from the guerrillas. In Vietnam the United States uproots the peasants from their homes and locks them into specially created strategic hamlets surrounded by barb wire to "keep out the Viet Kong."

The university administration decided to turn the entire university into one big strategic hamlet.

They created the category "nonstudent." By putting a "non" in front of the people hanging around Telegraph Avenue, they excluded us from the human race. It was like Germany inventing the term "non-Aryan." Anything bad that happened in Berkeley now could be blamed on the "nonstudent."

And of course, we, the nonstudents, dug the name. It was just what we'd been trying to say all along. We've given up on degrees, careers and all the external symbols of the Amerikan society.

We are proud to be known by what we are not.

To drive free spirits like Socrates Stew from the campus, the university administration issued an order making it illegal for nonstudents to sit at tables on campus without students beside them.

The university outlawed nonstudents leafleting on campus and said any organization with nonstudent members could not use university facilities.

The California State Legislature passed the Mulford Act: A nonstudent who does not leave the campus when ordered to by a university official can be arrested for trespassing.

To carry out all this pacification, the university mobilized a plainclothes cop with the fulltime job of walking around the campus in search of nonstudents, spying on politically active students, looking for rule violations, compiling dossiers and working closely with the Red Squad, FBI and CIA.

Stew spotted him and yelled out: "Hi there, Dean Fuzz!"

The name stuck.

The goal was to castrate students.

If students became politically active, they were kicked out of school and turned into "nonstudents." Mario Savio, the archetypal student leader, became a "nonstudent."

A student was defined as somebody with an enrollment card, not somebody interested in learning.

It was totalitarian state double-think.

But you had to feel some sympathy for the President of the University, Clark Kerr. He was so proud of his statistics and blueprints. The millions he panhandled from the Federal government and from big businessmen. The number of Nobel Prize winners at his university. The scores of buildings to be built. Weapons discovered. New departments. The football team.

But wherever Kerr traveled in the country, nobody asked him about his Nobel Prize winners or expansion programs. "What about those student demonstrators on campus?" they asked over and over again.

Poor Kerr. We stole his university right out from under his nose.

I was going to the Bear's Lair for a hamburger when I noticed a sit-in.

I can't resist a sit-in.

Whenever I see people sitting down, I suddenly get very tired.

Regardless of the issue—Biafra, lower pay for cops, blue skies, higher taxes. If you're sitting in and disrupting, I'll be there too.

After sitting down for an hour, I asked the guy next to me, "Hey, what's this sit-in all about anyway?"

It was a protest against *some* nonstudents who had put up a table outside the Bear's Lair and were handing out literature—an act absolutely forbidden by the new rules.

The students thought it was unfair for *these* nonstudents to hand out literature.

Being a nonstudent, I righteously agreed.

I picked up a piece of literature from this nonstudent table:

JOIN THE NAVY AND SEE THE WORLD

Some nonstudents are less "non" than others, especially military recruiters.

I sat through the entire sit-in without saying a word, getting ready any minute to leave for that hamburger.

Finally the cops arrived and surrounded the 1000 people sitting in. Berkeley Executive Vice Chancellor Earl F. Cheit, having just returned from a six-week refresher course in the Soviet Union, issued a statement *blaming the sit-in on six nonstudents*. The cops had arrest warrants for the six: Mario Savio, Stew Albert, Steve Hamilton, Mike Smith, Bill Miller and myself. Karen Wald, another nonstudent sitting right in the middle of the group, was ignored. Furious, she shouted, "You fucking male supremacists, arrest me, too!"

They led the six of us away and charged us with trespassing and public nuisance.

But the sight of cops on campus again infuriated all the moderate students, and the next day 8000 people swarmed onto the campus square to endorse nonstudent Mario Savio's call for a strike.

I dug it. The university's attempt to cast us as guerrilla fighters and the students as "dupes" built the *nonstudent myth* to gargantuan proportions. It insulted the students and increased their desire to drop out.

When you become a nonstudent, sex is better and more plentiful, you smoke more grass, you're healthier and happier and you grow 100 feet tall.

Melvin Belli, who had just defended Jack Ruby, wanted to take our case for free. I wanted to meet Belli.

We all went over to his San Francisco office. Belli told us he thought the Vietnam war was right.

Belli was a good liberal though. He said that the freedoms we were fighting for in Vietnam were lost on the campus when we were arrested. He believed the university should allow all political activity by students and nonstudents alike.

Belli wore cowboy boots and a new suit every day of the trial. His face was orange from the make-up he wore for the TV cameras.

His charisma dominated the courtroom. At one point in the middle of a motion to the judge, he theatrically pulled out a handkerchief and while the jury, the packed courtroom, the prosecutor and the judge hung in suspense, he took 40 seconds to blow his nose. We listened in total silence.

HONK! HONK!

Belli finished and said, "Excuse me, judge."

The cops testified that I did not play a leadership role in the sit-in.

Dean Fuzz said, "I don't think Jerry Rubin talked all day, *but he did smile a lot.*"

Belli then put Dean Cheit on the stand. Belli asked him, "You say that these people disrupted the normal processes of the university, Mr. Dean?"

The Good Dean replied, "Yes, they did."

Belli: "Did Jerry Rubin disrupt the normal processes of the university when he smiled?"

Belli's summation to the jury turned our necks red. "I can defend capitalism better than any man here," he began.

He appealed to the jury to affirm Amerikan democracy. "These are fine young men, and if you send them to jail, you only prove that they are right when they say that their government is evil."

We accidentally let onto the jury a dude who recently escaped as a refugee from Hungary. He took copious notes throughout the trial and became foreman and executioner on the jury.

After ten hours of deliberation the verdicts came down. We were all convicted of being public nuisances.

Mario got 90 days.

Stew got 60.

And I got the least, 45 days.

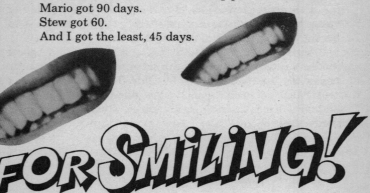

FOR SMILING!

6: Troop Trains Coming Through Our Town, Tra-la, Tra-la

Culver Pictures

"Troop trains coming! Troop trains! Choo! Choo!"

I heard professors Steve Smale and Moe Hirsch chugging through the Vietnam Day Committee house, out of breath. They pointed excitedly to a sentence in the back pages of the Berkeley *Gazette*: "City Council has approved Santa Fe's request to take troop trains through the city of Berkeley on their way to the Oakland Army Terminal."

Trains hauling GI's to Vietnam passing right through the residential area of our town! It was too much! The tracks were only five blocks from the VDC house.

Two VDC peace commandos jumped into a car and headed north 200 miles on an espionage mission. As soon as they saw a train, they were to telephone us. Then the VDC would flip into action.

We had a telephone tree. We'd call 10 people who would, in turn, call 10 people. Within an hour, 1,000 people could be mobilized by phone.

We printed leaflets proclaiming, "*Stop the Train!*" and painted picket signs.

Our table on campus was placed on Instant Demonstration Alert.

First day. No call from up north.

Another day. Still no call.

Then: "*I saw it! A train full of soldiers heading down to Berkeley!*"

VDC red lights flashed. All forces into motion. Within two hours 300 people stood waiting for the train, stretching a huge banner across the tracks: STOP THE WAR MACHINE.

Not a cop in sight. We expected that when the train crew saw so many of us on the tracks, they would brake the train to a grinding stop. What else could they do? We expected to stop the war machine.

The tracks started shaking. And there it was, a big fucking train rumbling toward us. Closer and closer. We stood our ground.

The train wasn't slowing down at all.

"*It's not going to stop!*"

"*Watch out!*"

We dived out of the way as the train roared past, slashing right through the banner.

The next day another call: another train is on its way. We alerted the press.

This time hundreds of us *sat* down on the tracks. Thirty cops formed a flying wedge to drive us off. We dashed to another spot and sat down again.

Surely the train will *stop* rather than *kill* human beings. But the train carrying the soldiers plunged through at full speed, escorted by a wedge of cops.

We stood at the side shouting at the train. A soldier at a window flashed the V-sign.

"*Did you see that?*"

Other soldiers held crudely made signs out of the window:

"LUCKY CIVILIANS."

"I DON'T WANT TO GO; KEEP IT UP!"

Gradually the full implications hit us. The Santa Fe railroad and the United States government were prepared to kill us rather than stop their bloody trains. We began to understand what War Machine meant.

But dig the signs the soldiers held! Our determination mounted. We'd stop that fucking train!

What to do?

Some people suggested dynamite. One guy suggested that we stall a car on the tracks and let the train smash into it.

We decided to bring more people to the tracks. We would force the train to stop by creating even more spectacular confrontation between the **Military** and *Human Life*.

We flooded Berkeley with thousands of "STOP THE TRAIN!" leaflets.

STOP
the
TROOP TRAIN!

The press speculated about the VDC's incredible intelligence. We knew when the trains were coming before the police knew. We notified the press about coming trains. How did we know?

We just winked, keeping everybody guessing, while VDC commandos kept their around-the-clock vigil waiting for the train.

The call came at 3 A.M. this time. So they were bringing the trains in early to try to fake us out. But we were ready.

At 6 A.M. 1000 people milled on the tracks, huddling together and sipping coffee to keep warm. About 50 Berkeley cops and dozens of plainclothes cops formed wedges to control us. We were trapped in a police box.

An idea: We could stampede down the tracks to meet the train.

On cue, everybody ran.

The cops chased.

TV cameramen with their heavy equipment were caught completely by surprise, but they lumbered off after us too.

For a mile demonstrators, cops and TV men stretched out, all running toward the train that would kill rather than stop.

The chance of somebody getting killed ran high.

Then the train appeared.

The engineer sprayed clouds of steam 20 feet in front of the train to drive people off the tracks. That meant that he could not see anyone on the tracks.

The steam blinded the people watching the advancing locomotive.

Plainclothes cops barreled down the tracks in front of the train to club people off.

35

A man lay face-down on the tracks.

People kneeled over him, pleading with him to get off.

He didn't respond.

One person tried to pull him off.

Impossible.

He called for more help, and two people tried to pull him off.

The train rumbled closer and closer.

Finally four people hauled on him.

At the last second he was pulled free, just as the train roared past.

Fighting broke out between cops and demonstrators all over the tracks.

One VDC guerrilla jumped on the back of the train and pulled the airbrake. Thirty others leaped aboard, and several clambered up onto the roof. Three demonstrators pushed into the last car and were thrown off by military police.

As demonstrators boarded the train, it began to slow up.

Then it crawled.

We formed ranks again across the tracks, as cops continued to try to shove us off.

The train stopped!!!

Cops tried to arrest those who had jumped on. As they moved to grab people, we split in all directions—only three or four were caught.

We ran, yipping and whooping, away from the tracks and through the streets, like a bunch of crazy motherfuckers.

We were victorious warriors.

We were ecstatic.

We had stopped the troop train.

We stopped the War Machine dead in its tracks.

7: It's Gotta Be More Fun to Be In the Revolution Than Out of It

The first decision was to keep the icebox full of beer at all times.

If you were lonely, you could always boogie on down to the Vietnam Day Committee house and find somebody to talk to.

If you had a scheme to save the world, you could always find someone to listen to you.

Any lunatic could walk in off the street, write a leaflet, mimeograph it, sign it "Vietnam Day Committee" and pass it out.

Wanderers passing through Berkeley ended up at the VDC, and many of them never got out of town.

Students stopped off and never went back to school.

Kids ran away from home and hid out at the VDC.

The phone was always ringing, sometimes all five at once. It was a trip just to answer them.

Anybody who wanted to know anything—how to bake a cake, how to get rid of Venereal Disease—would dial the VDC. We ran up bills of $2000 a month calling all ends of the earth to mobilize people against the war in Vietnam.

The VDC was born while organizing the biggest teach-in in the history of the world, Vietnam Day, a 36-hour happening attended by 50,000 different people. That experience taught us to believe in the *Apocalyptic Action*.

History could be changed in a day. An hour. A second. By the right action at the right time.

Our tactic was exaggeration. Everything was "the biggest," "the most massive."

Our goal was to create crises which would grab everybody's attention and force people to change their lives overnight.

VDC reconnaissance missions searching through the hills of Berkeley's grassy Tilden Park found secret kennels where the Army was training killer war dogs.

VDC commando/artists put up signs:

> **CAUTION: Army War Dogs in This Area. Keep Children and Pets Within Sight. If Dog Approaches Do Not Move.**
>
> U.S. Army, Official

Mothers and little kids dropped their picnic baskets and fled when they saw the signs. Near freakout.

The Army vigorously denied putting the signs up and said the dogs were fenced and under supervision. But three weeks later the kennels and dogs had disappeared. Victory!

We were putting out a weekly newspaper, organizing door-to-door discussions about Vietnam in the black ghetto in Oakland, sending out speakers everywhere, leafleting soldiers at airports telling them to desert, advising young kids how to beat the draft, and co-ordinating research, petition drives, massive and mini-demonstrations. No government official could come to the Bay Area without being haunted by a VDC reception team of psychic terrorists.

There were always hundreds of people packed into five rooms, committee meetings going on everywhere and crazy activists who craved trouble planning super-secret projects in back rooms. In one room crazies planned to rent planes and fly over the Rose Bowl dropping antiwar leaflets on the crowd. In another room crazier people planned a direct assault on the Oakland Army Terminal.

The VDC was an emotional hothouse, perpetually in orgasm. It was no place to meditate.

The VDC became a legend across the world.

If you were *not with* us, you were *against* us.

We knew the day was not far off when there'd be Nuremberg Trials in Amerika and we'd be the judges.

We were fucking obnoxious—and dug every moment of it.

8: "A Movement That Isn't Willing to Risk Injuries, Even Deaths, Isn't for Shit"

THOUSANDS OF STUDENTS AND OTHERS WILL BLOCK THE GATES OF THE OAKLAND ARMY TERMINAL AND SHUT IT DOWN!

The politicians picked up our threat. They declared a State of Emergency and ordered the National Guard on alert. That organized our demonstration for us! Everybody came to Berkeley for the action.

Steve Smale, co-chairman of the VDC, went on TV to reveal the plans. What tzuris Smale caused the university! One of the world's most famous mathematicians and the most renowned professor at the university, here was Smale plotting and working with nonstudent crazies!

Smale said that the VDC would attack the Terminal by air (dropping leaflets from planes), sea (thousands of oarsmen in rowboats) and land (10,000 people marching from the campus through Oakland to the Terminal).

The governor replied that police dogs, tear gas and 3,600 troops would be ready to repel the invaders.

Meanwhile, across the country anti-war groups mobilized for action—the first International Days of Protest against the war in Vietnam. Demonstrations on the same day in every city in the country! From New York to Berkeley, everyone got ready for simultaneous orgasm.

Were Minutemen going to stand on rooftops and shoot into the crowd of Berkeley peace marchers?

Suspense dominated Telegraph Avenue.

Watts had burned only two months earlier.

SHOWDOWN!

The teach-in was a bore. Too many words and not enough people. Only 4,000 were there, and our hearts sank.

But suddenly by seven o'clock that night, the campus was mobbed. Thousands of young people were pouring in from every direction. The largest crowd for a demonstration in the history of Berkeley!

Over 20,000 people!

The threats of the cops had not intimidated us!

We were going to end the war!

The teach-in speeches were still going on while the masses poured into the streets and began marching. The steering committee was caught on stage with its pants down, and committee members raced down side streets in an attempt to get in front of the marchers and lead them.

Ahead was the Oakland city limits and Oakland cops standing shoulder-to-shoulder across the street, armed with tear gas, clubs and police dogs.

As the march ebbed within three blocks of the war zone, the back of the line had not yet left the Berkeley campus. A massive line of humanity for 1½ miles from the campus to Oakland!

We were the bravest people in the whole world, our arms linked, singing, joyous.

Rumors filtered back:

"They got gas! They're going to tear gas us!"

None of us had ever been tear gassed before.

Debate broke out within the steering committee: what to do? turn left into Oakland? sit down? charge the lines? turn right back to Berkeley?

Behind us people shouted: *"Turn left! Turn left! Oakland! Oakland!"*

"We can't turn back," I said. *"This is the greatest night in Amerikan history!"*

"If we don't turn back, people are going to die. It'll destroy the movement forever!" said one Steering Committee member.

"If we turn back, it will destroy the movement!" Smale shouted.

"I don't want responsibility for somebody's death. We'll all be arrested. You can't run a movement from jail," another member said.

The chanting behind us grew louder: *"Left! Left!"*

"That's the fucking militants up front. They don't care what happens to the people behind them."

"Let's leave it up to the crowd," a militant said. *"The nine of us can't decide for 20,000 people. Let's stop the*

41

march, get the loudspeaker and let the people debate what to do."

"That's completely demagogic. How can you have democracy in the streets with 20,000 people when you're going to be tear gassed any minute? The people who shout the loudest will get their way," replied the spokesman for the conservatives.

The chanting grew more insistent: TURN LEFT! TURN LEFT! TURN LEFT!

"People may be killed. I don't want the responsibility."

"*A movement that isn't willing to risk injuries, even deaths, isn't for shit. We can't turn back because we're afraid someone may be killed.*"

The vote was 5-4 to turn back to Berkeley.

The banner swung to the right.

I fell back into the crowd, tears welling in my eyes.

Shock and puzzlement swept through the crowd. "What happened? This isn't the way to Oakland! Why are we going back to Berkeley!"

The joy and ecstasy that had rippled from soul to soul as we marched toward Oakland disappeared.

It became a funeral march.

Sad and solemn.

Fuck "leaders." Fuck "steering committees."
A movement that isn't willing to risk injuries, even deaths, isn't for shit.

The next day 8,000 people showed up for a second try, this time in the afternoon. As we approached the line of Oakland cops, someone whispered "The Hell's Angels are at the line."

Allen Ginsberg, clanging cymbals and singing *Hare Krishna* on the truck that headed the march, was worried. "I hope there won't be trouble," he said. "They're probably there to fight the police."

"Amerika first! Amerika for Amerikans! Go back to Russia, you fucking Communists!"

A blackjacketed Angel grabbed the banner at the head of the march and ripped it in two.

Fighting broke out all over between Angels and monitors. Panic. Monitors pleaded with the crowd, "Don't run. Sit down."

Club-swinging Berkeley cops moved in. One cop swung

43

from left field and split open the head of a 300-pound, 6-foot, 6-inch Angel. Blood spurted.

Another Angel jumped a cop and broke his leg.

But the Angels were outnumbered and finally captured. They were loaded one by one into paddy wagons, and the peace marchers cheered the Berkeley cop with the broken leg as he was carried off in a stretcher.

*　　*　　*

We vowed to march again on the Army Terminal in three weeks. But the overwhelming question was, "What if the Angels attack again?"

One night the Marxist left packed the VDC meeting and passed a resolution advocating arming and defending ourselves with clubs and defense guards.

The next night pacifists packed the meeting and passed a resolution saying, "If attacked, we will bleed."

Ginsberg came to the meetings with his own ideas:

we should announce in advance that psychologically less vulnerable groups like Women for Peace, grandmothers, naked girls, mothers, families and babies will be at the front of the march. If the Angels attack, everyone on the march should begin mass calisthenics.

we should immediately, en masse, sing "Three Blind Mice" or "Mary Had a Little Lamb."

at the first sign of disturbance, we should play over the PA system: "I Wanna Hold Your Hand."

every marcher should bring flowers and give them to the Angels, the police, the politicians and the press.

the march should include huge floats: Christ with the sacred heart and cross, Thoreau behind bars, Hell's Angels with halos.

"A demonstration is a theatrical production," Ginsberg said. "The life style, energy and joy of the demonstration can be made into an exemplary spectacle of how to handle situations of anxiety and fear/threat."

Could we get Dylan to come and sing at the march? Ginsberg pondered for a second and said, "Dylan might come if the march says nothing about the war. Like if everyone carries a placard with a picture of a different kind of fruit."

Nobody knew how to handle Ginsberg's pre-yippie, acid ideas.

Oakland again denied a march permit. But a federal

judge worked out a compromise: we couldn't close down the Oakland Army Terminal, but we could march to an Oakland park for a rally.

The Hell's Angels called a press conference. They announced they were going to spend the day getting drunk.

So the march came and went.

Twenty thousand people walked into Oakland with picnic baskets to hear after-dinner speakers in a march protected, ironically enough, by the Oakland cops.

The Oakland Mayor praised VDC monitors for their "responsible work."

Then all the people went their separate ways home.

The energy drained from the antiwar movement.
The VDC house rattled like an old skeleton.
One day a bomb blew half the building away.
The spirit once ours was restored to Mother Earth.

During the next two years, we tripped, made love and got to know ourselves, to prepare for our next life-or-death struggles against the war-makers: Oakland Stop the Draft Week and the Pentagon.

Meanwhile the war went on.

9: Any Fool Can Run for Mayor

Any fool with 25 signatures and $25 can run for mayor of Berkeley.

So I decided to run.

What better way to make fun of the political system than to run for public office?

We'll hold a marijuana teach-in in front of the police station and give joints to the cops as the campaign's main action.

We'll lead a march of 10-year-olds to the ballot box demanding the right to vote.

If elected I will not serve. We'll have a rotating mayorship, with everyone taking turns as mayor for a day.

We'll take over City Hall the way Castro took over the Havana Hilton.

I ran around Telegraph Avenue asking people what they thought of the idea.

"You mayor? Hah, hah, hah!" Everyone just started laughing.

That was exactly the reaction I wanted.

I'd just been arrested for being a public nuisance on the Berkeley campus, and I proclaimed that if elected I would pardon myself—and everybody else—in a public celebration.

Berkeley is a small Amerikan town with a revolution on its hands. Its mayor is a bald-headed Republican businessman who opened a business one day and worked and worked and worked and worked until he got employees, and then he worked and worked and worked until it became successful.

Mayor Wallace Johnson represents "the other Berkeley"—the Berkeley of bankers, retired military men and thousands of grandmothers in tennis shoes. The Berkeley with a Chamber of Commerce, the Amerikan Legion and Boy Scouts.

The Berkeley that was content and prosperous all of those years. Until all of a sudden it looked up and discovered anarchy, insanity, sex, drugs and rebellion in its midst. The town became the center of the world revolution.

Our campaign attacked Babbit's Berkeley. We began by infiltrating his little factory, Upright Scaffolding. A campaign worker went to the factory and applied for a job. He was hired. He spent the first two days counting faces— they were all white. The next day we shocked the community with a picket line in front of the Mayor's factory calling him a racist—running a Jim Crow business—in the middle of black Berkeley.

The embarrassed mayor put his foot in his mouth when questioned about racism in his factory: "It's my *private* business. It is not public information."

The nice thing about running for public office is that you get to speak before church groups, PTA, businessmen's associations and patriotic groups—at the same podium as your opponent.

Every time I appeared with Johnson, I launched a hair-raising personal attack on him. I called him a racist dog.

Capitalistic pig.

Coward.

Gutless politician.

Schmuck.

48

Johnson got up in the middle of one of the attacks and said: "I will not hear any abuse like this." He stalked out of the room. Just as the door slammed, I turned to the audience at the Women's Club:

"Now is that the way you want your mayor to behave?"

Everybody kept asking me: "Are you serious? Are you serious?"

In electoral politics "serious" means one thing:

Do you have any chance to win?

Maybe I could win?

The only other candidates in the race were a Trotskyite and a John Bircher. The Democrats were supporting Johnson.

I began to put together plans for victory—my winning combination. I'd get the votes of the students and nonstudents, if they'd register to vote. The black community —in opposition to racism at Johnson's factory. Then, finally, all those middle-class liberals who live high in the Berkeley hills. They want to see the Vietnam war end, but they also want to keep their nice view of the world. Who would they vote for—a prowar businessman or an antiwar public nuisance?

The campaign began to send people door-to-door throughout the whole fucking city, talking to people about the mayoralty election.

We learned an incredible truth.

Most people didn't even know they *had* a mayor.

Few knew his name.

No one knew what he looked like.

We, the radicals, had to go through the community convincing people that a good mayor made a difference, that votes and elections meant something, that democracy could work.

Stew and I slaved for a week writing a program with proposals on every issue. We scraped up $5,000 and printed 40,000 beautiful, psychedelic 25-page booklets—probably the most elaborate political program any candidate for office in Amerika has ever distributed.

I spent every day at the supermarkets handing them out and saying to people, "My name's Jerry Rubin. I'm running for mayor of Berkeley. Hope you'll vote for me."

A meeting of campaign workers voted down the idea of the rotating mayor because "nobody will vote for a candidate who says he's not going to serve if elected."

The marijuana teach-in was dropped.

I bought a vest and a gold suit.

I got a haircut and trimmed my mustache.

I lay awake nights asking myself whether I was serious.

"My name's Jerry Rubin. I'm running for mayor. Hope you'll vote for me."

"My name's Jerry Rubin. I'm running for mayor. Hope you'll vote for me."

I almost had it down to a tune.

I'll never forget the look of total disappointment and amusement on Stew's face when he saw me for the first time in my suit, three weeks before election day. He crumbled up a piece of paper and threw it at me in disgust.

Relations between Stew and me became strained.

Nancy and I almost broke up because I kept pushing everybody to work so hard.

"Every minute is a lost vote."

I woke up at 6 A.M. and worked until 2 A.M. I wanted everybody to do the same. I saw relaxing as a personal attack on the campaign.

I started saying to people: "You're not serious."

I started kissing babies and shaking every hand I could catch. I had no time to get stoned.

I began to look at people as "votes."

The people who were voting for me were the finest people who ever walked the earth.

The people who weren't voting for me were enemies. People were either pro-Rubin or anti-Rubin.

I was never seen without my white shirt, long tie and new suit.

On election night I was super-confident. Then the votes started pouring in:

Johnson. Johnson. Johnson.

My heart sank. *Johnson. Rubin. Johnson. Johnson.*

My heart sank deeper.

There was a "Rubin" here and there. But I was getting creamed.

I finished second, 7385 votes, 22 percent and won four precincts, all in the campus community. I got slaughtered in the hills and got few votes in the black community.

I learned the hard way that you can't build a new society while scrounging for votes in elections.

I tried to get votes from the parents of kids I had been telling to drop out of school, smoke pot and fuck each other.

To succeed in electoral politics you must be dishonest. Our new society is honest.

Elections are built around individual candidates. Our new society is collective.

I repudiated my life-style to get straight votes.

I will never put on a gold suit and vest again.

Fuck electoral politics.

Live the revolution.

Stephan Shames

10: We Are All Human Be-ins

One day some Berkeley radicals were invited over to the Buddhist temple of some San Francisco hippies. We got high and decided to get the tribes of Haight-Ashbury and Berkeley together.

A Gathering of the Tribes. Golden Gate Park. Free music by all of the rock bands in the city.

The hippies were calling it a Human "Be-in."

Nobody knew what the fuck a Be-in was.

We got stoned on some outasight grass. One Berkeley radical asked: "What are going to be the demands of this demonstration?"

The hippies patiently explained to him that it wasn't a "demonstration" and that we were just going to *be* there.

"People will turn each other on."

"Only good vibes."

"But no demands."

The Berkeley radical kept demanding that there be demands. So somebody gave him a pencil and paper and told him to write some.

It got to be so heavy that one S.F. hippie jumped up and said, "There's got to be more love in this room: *Roll some more joints.*"

People in the streets knew something was up. They seemed to catch on right away. If it had been a political demonstration they would have asked, "What are the issues? What are the demands? Why should we go?"

But this time everybody knew.

The purpose was just to *be.*

Golden Gate Park:
Rock music.
Grass.
Sun. Beautiful bodies.
Paint.
Ecstasy. Rainbows. No strangers!
Everybody smiling. *No picket signs or political banners*.
Our nakedness was our picket sign.

We played out our fantasies like children. We were kids playing "grown-up games." You can be whatever you want to be when you're a kid.

We were cowboys and Indians, pirates, kings, gypsies and Greeks. It was a panorama of history.

The rock bands created a tribal, animal energy.

We were a religion, a family, a culture, with our own music, our own dress, our own human relationships, our own stimulants, our own media.

And we believed that our energy would *turn on the world*.

55

All of that energy in one place at one time was the Atom Bomb explosion of the youth culture.

The Be-in: a new medium of human relations. A magnet drawing together all the freaky, hip, unhappy, young, happy, curious, criminal, gentle, alienated, weird, frustrated, far-out, artistic, lonely, lovely people to the same place at the same time. We could see one another, touch one another and realize that *we* were not *alone*.

All of our rebellion was reaffirmed.

It was a new consciousness.

Instead of *talking* about communism, people were beginning to *live* communism.

The fragmented life of capitalist Amerika—the separation between work and play, school and fun, property and freedom—was reconstituted by the joyous celebrants.

Neither the civil rights movement, the Free Speech Movement or the antiwar movement achieved its stated goals. They led to deeper discoveries—that revolution did not mean the end of the war or the end of racism. Revolution meant the creation of new men and women.

Revolution meant a new life.

On earth.

Today.

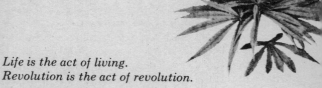

Life is the act of living.
Revolution is the act of revolution.

We are all human be-ins.

11 : HUAC Creates Subpoenas Envy and Meets Thomas Jefferson

"HUAC's giving out subpoenas! HUAC's giving out subpoenas!"

The word spread like fire.

"HUAC is investigating the Vietnam Day Committee!"

"Hey, wonder if I'll get one."

"Did you get one?"

"Let me see yours."

"Mine's bigger than yours."

"Wow!"

Those who got subpoenas became heroes. Those who didn't had *subpoenas envy*. It was almost sexual.

"Whose is bigger?"

"I want one, too."

"Let me see yours."

I went to a pay phone in the Berkeley Student Union to ask the Red Squad if I got a subpoena too. Just as I put the dime in, I felt a tap on my shoulder. It was Chick Harrison of the Berkeley Red Squad.

"Jerry Rubin," he said. "This is for you. A subpoena from the House Committee on Un-Amerikan Activities."

I snatched it out of his hands and ran through the Student Union, jumping up and down, clicking my heels together. It was the biggest, most beautiful subpoena in the world!

Within two hours I was on the steps of San Francisco City Hall in front of four television cameras, five photographers, four newspaper reporters, and seven radio stations, denouncing HUAC as a "witch-hunter."

I raved, "The government is trying to stifle antiwar dissent." The press hung on every word. I was playing Angry Radical, but inside I was laughing, standing on my hands and turning somersaults.

HUAC was not stifling dissent, but stimulating it—to greater and greater heights. People who did not get subpoenas were worried that they hadn't done enough against the war. "Haven't I sent enough blood to the Viet Kong?" I heard someone moan. "Haven't I burned enough draft cards? Organized big enough demonstrations?"

A fringe benefit of being a radical is occasional free trips to Washington to see your government in action. Remember when the third grade went off on those guided tours to visit Washington? Fuck guided tours. Become a subversive and see the government from the inside. Make your government pay your way there.

HUAC pays seven cents a mile. If you're coming from California that's almost twice the *youth fare:* which means you can live for two months free on HUAC's tab. HUAC finances the revolution!

A big meeting of subpoenaed witnesses, lawyers and others to discuss strategy turned into a generational struggle between the over-30's and the under-30's. Everyone over 30 put us on a down trip: If you try to do anything in front of HUAC, you will be cited for contempt of Congress and jailed for a year without appeal, they said.

Communist Party members and the National Committee to Abolish HUAC advised us to base the entire issue on the First Amendment and the right of dissent, a civil liberties fight. They wanted us to refuse to testify.

"FUCK YOU!" I yelled. "I'm not going to miss this opportunity to tell the world where it's at."

I never found the Amerikan people too uptight about the First Amendment anyway. The average baseball and football fans of Amerika can't be bored with legalistic

58

constitutional bullshit. We've got to be as exciting as the Mets.

"HUAC has destroyed reputations overnight and forced people to lose their jobs," said one member of the Communist Party.

Reputations? We had *no* reputations to lose. Jobs? We had *no* jobs to lose. How could HUAC hurt us? What names could they call us? Communists? Anarchists? Traitors? Motherfuckers? The worse the better.

The other subpoenaed witnesses were members of the Progressive Labor Party, and these were PL's daredevil, adventurist days. They planned to tell HUAC: "We are Communists and proud of it."

HUAC is a state of mind. It's only as powerful as your paranoia. If you're scared of it, it's 100 feet tall. If you laugh at it, the whole world laughs with you.

What were HUAC members going to do when they found themselves face-to-face with the biggest media freaks and publicity seekers since Jesus Christ?

I began thinking about HUAC as theater: I knew that I could not play on their stage, because they hold power in their gavel. I had to create my own theater to mindfuck HUAC and capture the nation's attention. But how?

I tossed out to Ronnie Davis of the San Francisco Mime Troupe the idea of coming to the hearings wearing the hat of an Amerikan Revolutionary War soldier.

"Why just the hat?" Ronnie asked. "Why not the whole uniform?"

BOOOOO

Lightning bolt!
HUAC as a Costume Ball.

A subpoenaed witness who wears a crazy costume to Congress would steal the show away from Joe Poole and his Cosmic Commie Killers. The unusual and the outrageous creates conversation, gossip, myth. And what if they force me to take my costume off?   ! ! ! !

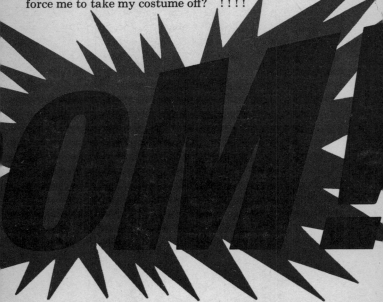

Most people I talked with tried to discourage me from wearing a crazy costume to Congress. The purpose of the hearings was to pass the Poole Bill through Congress, a bill which would make the things we were doing in Berkeley felonious crimes of treason punishable by twenty years in jail. "You'll make a fool of yourself," I heard over and over again. "Fool. Fool. Fool."

Where to get the costume? I called the nearest costume store, five blocks from my home in Berkeley. "Of course we have Amerikan Revolutionary war costumes." I put on the tricornered hat. Wow! My entire personality was transformed! Change a man's clothes and you change how he acts.

"How much?" I asked.

"$25 a week."

"It's a deal."

I wanted to give copies of the *Declaration of Independence* in parchment to each member of HUAC. You know the only place in the San Francisco-Berkeley area where we could find copies of the *Declaration of Independence?* The Amerikan Opinion Bookstore of the John Birch Society! Stew and I liberated their last few copies.

The day before the hearings were scheduled to open, our lawyers, Bill Kunstler, Arthur Kinoy and Beverly Axelrod, in a very untheatrical move, got a naive Washington, D.C. judge to stop the hearings on some constitutional technicality that I didn't understand.

But six hours later a higher court slapped the lower judge on the wrist and reversed the decision. So the performers, critics and the audience settled down to a Broadway opening.

I arrived at Congress in my costume, right down to the buckles over my shoes. I was so stoned that I was completely oblivious to the August heat in my wool uni-

form. Loaded down with leaflets and propaganda, I walked through the halls of Congress, past glowing TV cameras, sneering cops, curious secretaries of congressmen and hundreds of spectators until I reached the door of HUAC's hearing room where the head cop stopped me.

"It is against the law to pass out printed material in the halls of Congress," he said, huffing and puffing.

He tried to grab my leaflets.

"But it's my testimony," I screamed. Tug of war.

My beautiful lawyer, Beverly Axelrod, screamed, "Help! I'm an attorney for the witness, and the police won't let us in. Help!"

Nobody can resist a woman's screams. Poole, inside the hearing room, banged his gavel and ordered us in, literature, costumes and all. The floodlights and cameras buzzed. We were on stage.

I started walking around the HUAC hearing room, getting the feel of it: I was the only one appropriately dressed in the halls of Congress.

Our lawyers decided to get into the act. Kinoy, in his golden charismatic voice, repeatedly jumped up and gave Poole elementary lessons in law and life. Poole's neck grew redder as the hours wore on.

"You shut up!" Poole shouted.

Arthur kept going.

In an act that set the United States Congress back 100 years, Poole ordered three federal marshals to eject Kinoy from the room and arrest him.

What a trip to see three federal marshals, all big motherfuckers, grab 5-foot, 4-inch Arthur Kinoy and drag him out of the hearing room of the United States Congress. "This is the first time I've ever heard of a lawyer seized and charged with disorderly conduct while arguing a motion for a client," Arthur said later.

At that point each of our lawyers rose to give speech after speech and then to march out. That left us as clients without lawyers.

It was really tough on us clients.

Our fucking lawyers were upstaging us!

Leading witness for the government was Phillip Abbot Luce. I leaned over in my seat: I wanted to get a good look. I had seen Luce once before, two years earlier, at a press conference to discuss HUAC's plans to hold hearings on the Cuba trip. With a fiery, handlebar mustache, Luce had screamed, "There will be blood flowing at the halls of Congress, and it won't be our blood." Luce: the poet of the Progressive Labor Party.

Luce had changed sides. Dig it. Luce, who had helped organize the Cuba trips and had once gone skinnydipping with Fidel, joined with the FBI and ratted on all of his friends.

It was *the only* desertion in the history of our movement. Throughout the 1940's and the 1950's Communist Party members turned up as FBI agents. Every day right-wingers and liberals become left-wingers, radicals become yippies. But in the New Left there has been only one Phillip Abbot Luce.

His strange psychology fascinated me. PL said that he was a smack-head who had been blackmailed by threat of government prosecution. But I was eager to see him for myself.

He walked in from the back room; we "unfriendly" witnesses entered through the front. He had bought a brand new FBI-type blue suit for the hearings. He carried an attaché case with his initials on it. He was clean-shaven. Super-straight. He looked like every FBI agent you've ever seen in the movies.

As soon as he began, PL performers all over the room began shouting: "Let's stop this fink's testimony! He's a traitor! Fink! Traitor!" Marshals tried to clear the room. Scuffling broke out all over. The blood Luce promised two years earlier finally spilled, but he was on the other side.

The fighting subsided, twenty persons were arrested and then come the first words from Luce's mouth: "These people don't want a democratic dialogue."

Luce put us to sleep. His routine was so bloodless, sexless, mechanical and dull that it was evil. His speech could have been written by J. Edgar Hoover. *He was so much more interesting as a leftist.*

The right-wing and FBI probably pay him a lot of money as the Young Amerikans for Freedom's favorite after-dinner speaker. But the problem is that in Amerika you have to spend your time with the people who pay your salary. And right-wingers and FBI agents make pretty boring company.

When it came time for us crazies to testify, the theater switched to high comedy. Anatole Anton identified himself as James Bond. He called Poole "Jo-Jo" and the lawyer asking the questions "Mr. Lackey." Steve Cherkoss took the oath with what *The New York Times* described as a "raised fist with the middle finger uplifted." Stuart

McCrae gave the Nazi salute when he came to the stand. He began by saying that the hearing made him so sick, "I might vomit all over the table." Jeff Gordon shouted at Poole: "We are the comrades of the Amerikan soldiers. You and Johnson are their enemies because you have sentenced them to die." Asked when he was born, Steve Hamilton called them "yellow-bellied, racist cowards" and started giving the history of racist-fascist Amerika. He began a Congressional Fillibuster. He wouldn't shut up. He finally had to be dragged away from the witness stand. I awaited my turn, blowing giant bubbles with my bubble gum, whistling patriotic songs, making sarcastic remarks, jumping up and down.

Poole banged his gavel every two minutes. It was a circus, and he was barker.

After four days of hell-raising my turn came. I stood up.
Started to take the stand.
Poole stopped me.
He called the hearings off.
Federal marshals grabbed me by my arms and legs and started to carry me out of the hearing room.
"I wanna testify! I wanna testify!" I yelled.
I lost my tricornered hat in the scuffle and was charged with disorderly conduct. Joe McCarthy turned over in his grave.

The poor liberals were so embarrassed. The hearings embarrassed the "dignity of Congress."
The Poole Bill died in committee.

"Cess" Poole went back to Dallas, where he was greeted by cheering mobs.
We went back to Berkeley, where we were greeted by cheering mobs.
The crazies on the right and the crazies on the left had a great time.

12: Hollywood Casts the Peace Movement for the Battle of the Pentagon

Generational war flared within the Peace Movement in San Francisco on April 15, 1967. On the speaker's platform stood lifeless professors, ministers, Reform Democrats, union leaders, intoning speech after boring speech. Down in the street stood freeks, longhairs, beatniks, students, kids, the unwashed. Why were *we* standing around listening to *them?*

Country Joe and the Fish were cut off during their second song to make time for more speeches. We were pissed off.

The Peace Movement was trying to put on a respectable front to convince straight people that you don't have to have long hair to be against the war. The Peace Movement was still using pictures of napalmed babies to shame the public, despite the fact that CBS-TV was already doing it better—in color!—on Cronkite.

The Peace Movement was too fucking polite. Martin Luther King was only as powerful as the black man standing behind him with a molotov cocktail. "If you don't listen to me, you're going to have to deal with some mighty mean niggers." Antiwar pacifists are only as strong as crazy revolutionaries who are ready to burn the whole motherfucker down.

After the march I was going through one of my regular dropout "identity crises." Nancy and I prepared to hitch around the world as correspondents for the *Berkeley Barb*. As we were packing, Dave Dellinger called from New York: Would I come East to be project director for the National Mobilization's antiwar demonstration in Washington in October?

I went to New York.

"People in Berkeley think we ought to try to shut down the Pentagon this fall with massive civil disobedience," I told Dave. He grinned, a twinkle in his eye. He's in his early 50's, but he's a kid at heart, a born troublemaker. If there were a million Dave Dellingers, there'd be no generation gap.

"We considered that," Dave said, "but the Pentagon is in Virginia, across the bridges from Washington. All the government has to do is block the bridges, and we'd never reach the Pentagon."

United Press International, Inc.

Fuck! On the West Coast we had never considered the geographical problems. All we saw was a Hollywood spectacular: *Peace Movement Attacks Pentagon*.

Details can sure fuck up a great scenario. "Let's not let details get in the way of the myth," I said. "We gotta choose a symbol so evil that we can do anything we want and get away with it."

Five of us drove to Washington to check out the Pentagon. It was too much.

Our tourist guide boasted that it was the largest office building in the world: 17½ miles of corridors! The *business* of *genocide*. And, as with any other business, everybody does his little job within it.

We dedicated ourselves to bringing the consequences of their business right to their front door: B-L-O-O-D.

Our scenario: We threaten to close the motherfucker down. This triggers the paranoia of the Amerikan government: The Man then organizes our troops for us by denying us a place to rally and march. Thus just-another-demonstration becomes a dramatic confrontation between Freedom and Repression, and the stage is the world. After our people are organized, we soften our rhetoric and our massive numbers force the government to back down. *We end up seizing the Pentagon!*

68

Karl Bermann

We needed a spectacular press conference to grab the imagination of the world and play on appropriate paranoias. For that we needed the help of Amerika's baddest, meanest, most violent nigger—then H. Rap Brown. Rap's presence at the press conference, whether or not he even showed up at the Pentagon, would create visions of FIRE. Rap agreed to come.

We needed to fill out the script with the other right character actors—a Vietnam veteran, a priest, a housewife from Women Strike for Peace, a professor, an SDS leader and then such folks as Dick Gregory. Dave Dellinger was Leading Man, combining stirring guerrilla-war rhetoric with a kindly, benign appearance; he could be your Uncle Dave. Bob Greenblatt, national coordinator of the MOB and then a Cornell professor, lent the prestige of the academy. And my wild hair and handlebar mustache suggested the anarchist bomb-thrower, capable of *anything*.

We began the press conference by identifying the Peace Movement with the Detroit and Newark riots. The newsmen quickly asked Rap if he would bring a gun to the Pentagon.

He answered: "I'd be unwise to say I'm going with a gun because you all took my gun last time. *I may bring a bomb, sucker.*"

Col. Jerome Z. Wilson of the Strategic Air Command, posing as Abbie Hoffman, promised that a crowd of holy men would "surround the Pentagon, chanting and beating drums, and the Pentagon will rise into the air. When it reaches 300 feet, all the evil spirits will fall out." Col. Wilson, who had recently dropped out of SAC because of "bad vibrations," also revealed that marijuana, already planted on the Pentagon lawn, would be ready for harvest on October 21. "We will defoliate Washington's cherry trees and turn the Potomac River purple," he added.

"Thousands of people will fill the hallways and block the entrances to the Pentagon," I said. "We will bring a community of joy to a place whose only business is murder. We will then disrupt and dislocate all the major institutions of Amerikan society."

The press was great.

They picked up an offhand remark by Dave—"There will be no government building left unattacked"—and made pacifist Dave sound like a terrorist.

AP reported, "When asked if his followers would practice nonviolence in Washington, Rap Brown turned away without answering."

It added, "A spokesman for Defense Secretary McNamara had no comment."

The Pentagon was as good as in our hands!

But as usual it wasn't the Pentagon or the government which would fuck things up. It was the Peace Movement.

The Berkeley Crazies—Nancy, Stew, Karen Wald and I—put out the first issue of *Mobilizer* on behalf of the National Mobilization Committee; it was an internal newspaper to be mailed to peace groups across the country. We included Keith Lampe's article "On Making A Perfect Mess," which made suggestions like: "As the network camera wheels in for the classic counter-demonstrator footage, the BOMB PEKING signs will be flipped to say DOES LBJ SUCK? Eight thousand hippies will panhandle at embassies to create a certain international embarrassment. During a block party in front of the White House a lad of nine will climb the fence and piss, piss, piss."

The shit came down.

Women Strike for Peace representatives in the National Mobilization coalition turned into little old ladies in tennis shoes, screaming about "obscenity." "How can we hand out literature with words like this—suck, piss?" they bellowed at crisis meetings.

An influential MOB member was also an official of the Retail Sales Union. He flipped out over Keith's suggestion that "a thousand children will stage Loot-ins at department stores to strike at the property fetish that underlies genocidal war." He rose from his chair, ranting and raving: "How can I ask my men to come to this demonstra-

tion when you are going to loot department stores they work in?"

Our issue of *Mobilizer*, though 5,000 copies were already printed, was confiscated. It cost $50 to get a copy on the Peace Movement black market.

A new *Mobilizer* appeared with a prominent article entitled, "Sid Peck Answers the Questions of Housewives About the October 21 Demonstration." (He assured them they could bring along the kids and be home in time for supper.)

I was furious at the censorship within the Peace Movement. All over 40, they were planning a demonstration in which young kids, 15 to 25, would shed their own blood and go to jail, another one of those scenes where the old motherfuckers are on the platform and the kids in the stands.

Plans for shutting down the Pentagon were quietly de-emphasized, and the peaceful, legal march stressed. The old people in the MOB were after my ass.

I was considering doing what I tell everyone else to do—dropping out of the whole bureaucratic mess. Nancy already had, joining Abbie as a Digger on the Lower East Side. But in the middle of one of our most bitter feuds within MOB, our best friend united us. The United States government!

Ivy League Harry Van Cleve, a government lawyer selected by the Pentagon and police to negotiate with us, said that if we planned to "close down the Pentagon," the government would not issue permits for any rally or march.

It was Beatle music to our ears! *The government was following the script*, even if the Peace Movement wasn't.

Within two days Martin Luther King, Benjamin Spock and SDS were coming. They'd all been cool beforehand, King concerned with his own movement, Spock worried about possible violence, SDS viewing national demonstrations as a drain on local energies. The government settled the issue. Who could be cool to a demonstration the government was trying to prohibit?

The government must have had a shit-fit listening to our tapped phones. Van Cleve telephoned Dellinger to request another meeting. And for the next two weeks, in six meetings, the criminals negotiated with the government about the crimes we were going to commit. Van Cleve tried to win us over with kindness and warmth, treating each point technically. You would have thought we were discussing a merger between two corporations.

The government was trying out a new strategy to control the demonstration. Outright prohibition had failed, so Van Cleve was now playing the part of a skilled surgeon taking out a diseased body organ. His strategy was to take the drama out of the demonstration through a thousand little points in the negotiations.

He chopped away our starting and leaving times, gave us one bridge to Virginia instead of two, prohibited sound amplification at the Pentagon, and prevented us from arriving at the War Machine until 4:30 P.M.

Negotiations came down to the final day before the siege, and one issue was unresolved—the road from the bridge in Virginia to the Pentagon. We wanted the Washington-Jefferson Highway because you could see the Pentagon the entire way. The crowd's emotion would build as it marched closer. Because of "traffic" Van Cleve offered us only an out-of-the-way, winding undramatic road that arrived at the Pentagon from the side.

I argued that we should break off negotiations. Dave said, quite sensibly, "How do we explain to our people that they will be beaten and arrested at the bridges because we didn't like the road we got?"

Dellinger signed an agreement for us—scheduled lawbreaking! A demonstration with a beginning, middle and an end. Peace Movement people were coming from all over Amerika with round-trip bus tickets! A riot for middle-class commuters?

*   *   *

Ideal football weather brought tens of thousands pouring into town for The Big Game. The day before thousands of kids in Berkeley had rioted and closed down the Oakland draft board. The first white riot!

The newspapers spoke of the Pentagon demonstration in military language: mobilization, State of Emergency, troops deployed, showdown! LBJ had ordered the 82nd Airborne, veterans of other domestic troubles (Detroit, Newark, the Dominican Republic), to protect the Pentagon.

The Rally: Boring speeches. Inaudible sound system. Discovering old friends. A national demonstration is a reunion of friendships.

The Parade: We're in motion! Dignitaries up front. Slow down! Slow down!

Super Joel to Dr. Spock: "Hey, this march is going too slow for us speed freaks."

The word spreads: The soldiers at the Pentagon have bayonets.

We cross the bridge. Our "agreement" says we must rally and hear more speeches in the North Parking Lot until 4:30 P.M., but nobody at the demonstration knows that. We get closer to the Pentagon.

The Bettmann Archive

Charge!

Tear down a fence between the rally site and the hated building. The attack surges toward the Pentagon from three different directions.

The Bettmann Archive

Siege!

War between longhair peace demonstrators and helmeted soldiers with bayonets ignited all over. Demonstrators tried to smash their way through the troop lines to get at the building. We threw rocks, beer cans and garbage, and the soldiers clubbed us down with their rifle butts. The first blood ran at the Pentagon.

75

Two hundred of the bravest young men and women in the land, using their North Vietnamese flagpoles as clubs, broke through one line of soldiers and forced their way inside the building, *inside the Pentagon*. The U.S. Army could not keep peace demonstrators out of the Pentagon! The Pentagon was not invincible!

Rifle butts drove us back, twenty skulls cracked and blood flowing.

The demonstrators linked arms while the troops tried to club us away. "Hold that line! Hold that line!" We held and the Army stopped. The Army withdrew, accepting the line which we had won.

Victory!

Mel Zimmer

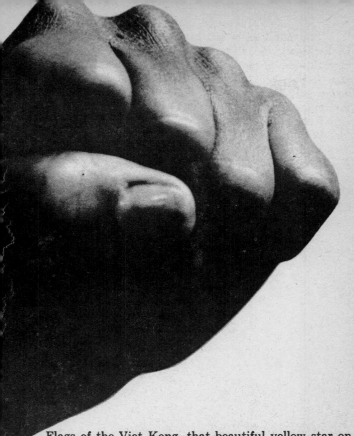

Flags of the Viet Kong, that beautiful yellow star on a red and blue field, waved high in front of the Pentagon!

Demonstrators snatched helmets from soldiers and ran back into liberated zones shouting, "Souvenir! A souvenir!"

Beautiful naked chicks went up to GI's and suggested that they take off their uniforms and come home with them.

Super Joel put a flower in the nozzle of one soldier's rifle.

We heard buses gunning their motors. The middle-class Peace Movement was going home. They left us tons of food; we were their troops. We settled down in front of the Pentagon for a long stay.

Every few minutes skirmishes flared. TV cameras ground away during every battle. Hourly bulletins flashed the Pentagon war to the world.

From a distance draft cards at dusk looked like fire-flies around the Pentagon.

Night fell.

Here we were, smelly, naked, hairy beasts—facing ranks of immobile soldiers before the theatrical backdrop of the Amerikan war machine.

The whole scene was bleached white by the unearthly glare of carbon-arc spotlights. (*It was the story of* Amerika *told in Biblical imagery.*)

We were smoking pot, passing joints from person to person, taking bites out of sandwiches and apples and passing them on. We huddled together to keep warm.

The soldiers had orders not to move a muscle or show any expression on their faces.

We shouted to the soldiers, "Join us! Join us!" We believed that they might throw off their helmets and come to our side. We had girls, pot, food, community warmth

and we weren't taking any orders. They were all regimented and controlled. It was the psychedelic vs. the linear, free vs. fixed, spontaneous vs. uptight.

Through Saturday night and Sunday, demonstrators took turns at the bullhorn talking to the soldiers. For 15 hours, the lumpen middle-class youth of Amerika poured out its heart to the Amerikan soldiers protecting the Pentagon. One guy broke down and cried, "My father is an officer in the army, and they're making him a murderer. I can't stand it!!!"

Rumors spread that three soldiers actually threw off their helmets and jumped to our side. We cheered the news. If we had stayed at the Pentagon another week, the entire 82nd Airborne would have deserted!

Stew took a turn at the bullhorn on Sunday afternoon and within a minute seized the soldiers' attention:

"We grew up in the same country, and we're about the same age. We're really brothers because we grew up listening to the same radio programs and TV programs, and we have the same ideals. It's just this fucked-up system that keeps us apart.

"I didn't get my ideas from Mao, Lenin or Ho Chi Minh. I got my ideas from the Lone Ranger. You know the Lone Ranger always fought on the side of good and against the forces of evil and injustice. He never shot to kill! . . .

"I went to PS 206 in Brooklyn, and when I was in school nobody liked strict teachers. We always hoped to get teachers who weren't strict. The government has become a super-strict teacher. We didn't like them when we were kids, so why should we like them now? We always considered the monitors to be finks, and now you guys are acting like monitors. Join us!"

U.S. marshals reached through the lines to grab and club some of us every few minutes. Fighting flared and then subsided. Rumors spread that within a half hour the soldiers would attack and massacre us on the Pentagon steps. We believed every rumor. Once during the night, after the TV crews went home, they did attack, arresting and clubbing a few hundred of us.

We looked around and saw who we were: the leftovers of 100,000 peace protesters. We were the scragglies, the raggedy bunch, longhairs, the white niggers of Amerikan society—and the white niggers of the Peace Movement.
We were scared but we had each other.

At midnight Sunday, 30 hours after our arrival, a mechanical Big Brother voice boomed from the Pentagon that all who stayed would be arrested. Huge vans rolled in.
We vowed that we would never again choose out of principle to get arrested, but we needed to complete the Pentagon demonstration theatrically.
The marshals and soldiers scooped 500 of us into vans within 15 minutes.

I was busted while engaging in a religious act, pissing on the Pentagon wall. It satisfied an immediate need and made a profound moral statement. I demanded they charge me with "urinating on the Pentagon," a political-sexual crime. Instead they booked me for "loitering," and I got 30 days in jail.

After they put us away, cleaning crews came in to clean up the rest of the garbage. They tried to clean up so well that the five o'clock Monday morning war shift would think nothing had happened. But our spray-painted CHE LIVES signs were invincible.

all the Man's machines
and all the Man's men
couldn't wash the blood
away in time.

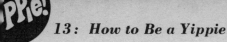

13: *How to Be a Yippie*

We got very stoned so we could look at the problem *logically*:

It's a *youth* revolution.

Gimme a "Y."

It's an *international* revolution.

Gimme an "I."

It's people trying to have meaning, fun, ecstasy in their lives—a *party*.

Gimme a "P."

Whattaya got?

Youth International Party.

Paul Krassner jumped to his feet and shouted: *"YIP-pie! We're yippies!"*

A movement was born.

All of us in the room that New Year's Eve knew, when we heard it, that in a few months "yippie" would become a household word.

Abbie, Anita, Paul, Nancy and I began jumping up and down all around the room, yipping.

Would people really call themselves yippies?

A few months earlier Dean Rusk came to town and we ran through the streets setting fires in trash cans, splashing blood onto passing limousines and disrupting traffic. As we ran, we shouted something that sounded like "yippie."

Yippie is the sound of surging through the streets.

Yippies—the name of a nonorganization, nonpolitical party—the Youth International Party. Also the actor in the party: a yippie! And the battle cry: **YIPPIE!**

Myths offer kids a model to identify with.

Amerika's myths—from George Washington to Superman to Tarzan to John Wayne—are dead. Amerikan youth must create their own myths.

A new man was born smoking pot while besieging the Pentagon, but there was no myth to describe him. There were no images to describe all the 14-year-old freeks in Kansas, dropping acid, growing their hair long and deserting their homes and their schools. There were no images

to describe all the artists leaving the prison of middle-class Amerika to live and create art on the streets.

The Marxist acidhead, the psychedelic Bolshevik. He didn't feel at home in SDS, and he wasn't a flower-power hippie or a campus intellectual. A stoned politico. A hybrid mixture of New Left and hippie coming out something different.

A streetfighting freek, a dropout, who carries a gun at his hip. So ugly that middle-class society is frightened by how he looks.

A longhaired, bearded, hairy, crazy motherfucker whose life is theater, every moment creating the new society as he destroys the old.

The reality was there. A myth was needed to coalesce the energy.

Yippies forged that myth and inspired potential yippies in every small town and city throughout the country to throw down their textbooks and be free.

Yippies would use the Democratic Party and the Chicago theater to build our stage and make the myth; we'd steal the media away from the Democrats and create the specter of "yippies" overthrowing Amerika.

The myth is real if it builds a stage for people to play out their own dreams and fantasies.

The myth is always bigger than the man. The myth of Che Guevara is even more powerful than Che. The myth of SDS is stronger than SDS.

The myth of yippie will overthrow the government.

The myth makes the revolution. Marx is a myth. Mao is a myth. Dylan is a myth. The Black Panthers are a myth.

People try to fulfill the myth; it brings out the best in them.

The secret to the yippie myth is that it's nonsense. Its basic informational statement is a blank piece of paper.

The left immediately attacked us as apolitical, irrational, acidhead freeks who were channeling the "political rebellion of youth" into dope, rock music and be-ins. The hippies saw us as Marxists in psychedelic clothes using dope, rock music and be-ins to radicalize youth politically at the end of a policeman's club.

The hippies see us as politicos and the politicos see us as hippies. Only the right wing sees us for what we actually are.

The slogan of the yippies is: *"Rise up and abandon the creeping meatball!"* The straight press thought that "creeping meatball" meant Lyndon Baines Johnson and that we wanted to throw him out of office.

We just laughed, because we love LBJ. LBJ was our leader, founder, guru. Where would we be without LBJ?

Everybody has his own creeping meatball—grades, debts, pimples. Yippies are a participatory movement. There are no ideological requirements to be a yippie. Write your own slogan. Protest your own issue. Each man his own yippie.

All you have to do to be a yippie is to be a yippie.

Yippie is just an excuse to rebel.

If you ask "Do yippies really exist?" then you're not a yippie.

If you say, "There are no yippies," you're not a yippie.

Last year's yippie is already respectable.

This year's yippie sucks.

Yippies are freaky so kids out there will say, "I can be freaky and get away with it, too."

When somebody gets further out than the yippies, then it's time to get further out than them, or dissolve the yippies.

Yippies believe there can be no social revolution without a head revolution and no head revolution without a social revolution.

There's no such thing as a YIPPIE FOLLOWER. There are 646½ million different kinds of yippies, and the definition of a yippie is that he is a LEADER. Yippies are *Leaders without followers*.

Yippies do whatever we want to do whenever we want to do it. Yippies know we're sane and everyone else is crazy, so we call ourselves "the crazies."

Yippies say if it's not fun, don't do it.

We see sex, rock 'n' roll and dope as part of a Communist plot to take over Amerika.

We cry when we laugh and laugh when we cry.

To be a yippie you got to watch color television at least two hours a day, especially the news.

The yippie idea of fun is overthrowing the government.

Yippies are Maoists.

Yippies are put-ons because we make our dreams public.

We will avenge the murder of Che.

Reporter: Where do the yippies get their money?

Yippie: Did you ever ask the Pope where he got his ring?

85

Yippies are city freeks. We feel at home in a traffic jam.

The left demands full employment for all—we demand full unemployment for all. The world owes us a living!

Straights shit in their pants when they hear the yippies reveal the most crucial political issue in Amerika today: pay toilets.

Yippies want to run naked through the halls of Congress.

The yippies hold secret strategy meetings with Ronnie Reagan to plan how to radicalize Berkeley students.

Yippies get stoned on Fidel's speeches.

We started yippie with an office, a mailing list, three telephone lines, five paid staff organizers, weekly general meetings and weekly Steering Committee meetings. We were the hardest workers and most disciplined people you ever met, even though we extol sloth and lack of discipline. We are a living contradiction, because we're yippies.

Marijuana is compulsory at all yippie meetings.

Yippies take acid at breakfast to bring us closer to reality.

Holden Caulfield is a yippie.

The Old Nixon was a yippie; the New Nixon is not.

Yippies believe every nonyippie is a repressed yippie. We try to bring out the yippie in everybody.

Yippies proclaim: *Straights of the world, drop out! You have nothing to lose but your starched shirts!*

The revolution will come when everybody is a

14: Our Leaders Are Seven-Year-Olds

Amerika says: **Don't!**
The yippies say: **Do It!**

Everything the yippies do is aimed at three-to-seven-year-olds.

We're child molesters.

Our message: Don't grow up. Growing up means *giving up your dreams*.

Our parents are waging a genocidal war against their own kids. The economy has no use or need for youth. Everything is already built. *Our existence is a crime.*

The logical next step is to kill us. So Amerika drafts her young niggers and sends us to die in Vietnam.

The function of school is to keep white middle-class youth off the streets. *High schools and colleges are fancy baby-sitting agencies.*

Vietnam and the school system are the two main fronts in Amerika's genocidal campaign against the youth. Jails and mental hospitals follow closely.

Amerika says: *History is over.* Fit in. The best system in the history of man has been discovered—it's yours. Nothing else is possible because man is selfish, greedy, tainted by Original Sin. If we don't fit in, they lock us up.

But for the masses of people throughout the world, history is just beginning. We kids want to start again too, rebuilding from scratch.

We want to be heroes, like those we read about in the history books. We missed the First Amerikan Revolution. We missed World War II. We missed the Chinese and Cuban Revolutions. Are we supposed to spend our futures grinning and watching TV all the time?

A society which suppresses adventure makes the only adventure the suppression of that society.

Republican fat-cat businessmen see their kids become SDS leaders. War profiteers' children become hippies. Senators' kids are arrested at pot parties.

Generational war cuts across class and race lines and brings the revolution into every living room.

The revolution toppled the high schools in 1968. Soon it will go to the junior highs and then the grade schools.

The leaders of the revolution are seven-year-olds.

15: Don't Trust Anyone Over 40

"DON'T TRUST ANYONE OVER 30."

Thus spake Jack Weinberg, and 2,000 people at a Free Speech Movement rally in Berkeley rose to their feet.

The generation gap was born.

Everybody agreed with FSM's goals. But some people said: "Be patient and go through channels." Others screamed: "I can't sit still!"

Suddenly we realized what was going down. Instead of wasting time asking someone what his political position was, all you had to ask was his age.

Those over 30 snuggled up against the status quo, youthful ideals behind them. They were in a leaky rowboat on a stormy sea. "Quit rocking the boat," they said.

But soon "Don't trust anyone over 30," the proud radical slogan, was taken over by the conservatives. The over-30's said: "Wait till you reach 30; you'll be just like us." They saw the movement as an adolescent stage one passed through on his way to the suburbs.

Some of us reached the age of 30. We didn't grow up.

We say: "Don't trust anyone over *40!*"

We're permanent adolescents.

We reject careers and middle-class rowboats.

Our culture, the hippie longhair culture, is ageless. Forty-, 30-, 20- and 10-year-olds live together on the same street corners.

Age—what's age?—we don't even carry a watch.

No one ever asks a fellow longhair how old he is. It's a counterrevolutionary question. Long hair and beards make everyone look the same age.

When we're 35, our ambition is to act like we're 15.

We know each other by *first* names.

We live *now*.

Liberals like *The Village Voice* and Mayor Daley use the same weapon to attack the yippies: our age.

"They're just a bunch of 30-year-olds trying to mislead Amerikan youth," they chorus.

We laugh when we hear that because we've discovered the fountain of youth. You're only as old as you wanna be. Age is in your head.

We're born twice.

It's your second birth—your *revolutionary* birth—which is the important one.

I was born in the FSM in Berkeley in 1964.

That makes me five years old!

When *The Village Voice* and Daley say, "Don't trust anyone over 30," I reply:

I got 25 more years!

Growing up means collecting garbage. Staying young means throwing out as much garbage as you collect. I'm for lowering the voting age to 5 and prohibiting old people over 40 from voting unless they can puke up all of their garbage.

One of the yippiest yippies is Bertrand Russell, who participated in his first sit-in when he was over 90 calendar years old. Nikita Khrushchev, 60, as premier of Russia, banged his shoe on a table at the United Nations during a childish temper tantrum. You can be a yippie no matter how old you are!

You can't use your physical age as a cop-out.

The 1950's were the turning point in the history of Amerika. Those who grew up before the 1950's live today in a mental world of Nazism, concentration camps, economic depression and Communist dreams Stalinized. A pre-1950's child who can still dream is very rare.

Kids who grew up in the post-1950's live in a world of supermarkets, color TV commercials, guerrilla war, inter-

national media, psychedelics, rock 'n' roll and moon walks. For us *nothing is impossible. We* can do *anything.*

This generation gap is the widest in history. The *pre-*1950's generation has *nothing* to teach the *post-*1950's, and that's why the school system is falling apart.

The pre-1950's generation grows more desperate. We dreamers disturb straight Amerika's dreamless sleep.

They were alive when Germany created concentration camps for Jews and other troublemakers.

Will they send us, their own children, to concentration camps?

16: Long Hair, Aunt Sadie, Is a Communist Plot

My earliest introduction to Communism involved family intrigue and outasight chicken soup. Every family has a black sheep. Mine was Aunt Sadie in New York.

"She went to Russia to meet Stalin," members of the family used to gossip to each other.

When I was a kid, my family often visited Aunt Sadie, and she served the best chicken soup in the whole world. She used to say to me, "**Jerry**, you must still be hungry. Please eat some more, **Jerry darling**. Eat some more good chicken soup."

And as she ladled more chicken soup into my already overflowing bowl, she'd whisper into my ear, "The capitalists need unemployment to keep wages down."

I lost contact with Aunt Sadie and meanwhile became a family misfit myself. Then one unexpected afternoon Aunt Sadie knocked on the door of my Lower East Side apartment. I hadn't seen her in ten years.

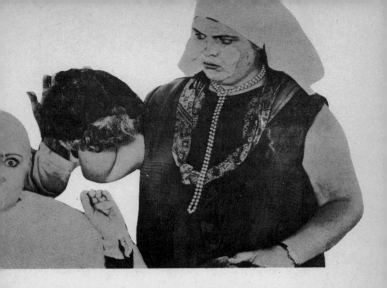

"Aunt Sadie," I shouted, hugging her. "I'm a commie, too!"

She didn't even smile.

Maybe she was no longer a Communist?

"Aunt Sadie, what's the matter?"

She hesitated. "**Jerry**, why don't you cut your hair?"

So I gave her a big bowl of Nancy's outasight chicken soup and began:

"Aunt Sadie, long hair is a commie plot! Long hair gets people uptight—more uptight than ideology, cause long hair is communication. We are a new minority group, a nationwide community of longhairs, a new identity, new loyalties. We longhairs recognize each other as brothers in the street.

"Young kids identify short hair with authority, discipline, unhappiness, boredom, rigidity, hatred of life—and long hair with letting go, letting your hair down, being free, being open.

93

"Our strategy is to steal the children of the bourgeoisie right away from the parents. Dig it! Yesterday I was walking down the street. A car passed by, parents in the front seat and a young kid, about eight, in the back seat. The kid flashed me the clenched fist sign."

"**But, Jerry** . . ." Aunt Sadie stammered.

"Aunt Sadie, *long hair is our black skin.* Long hair turns white middle-class youth into niggers. Amerika is a different country when you have long hair. We're outcasts.

We, the children of the white middle class, feel like Indians, blacks, Vietnamese, the outsiders in Amerikan history."

"**But, Jerry**," Aunt Sadie interrupted, "the Negroes in the ghettos, they're only hurting themselves. I mean, all of the vandalism and everything . . ."

"Long hair polarizes every scene, Aunt Sadie. It's instant confrontation. Everyone is forced to become an actor, and that's revolutionary in a society of passive consumers.

"Having long hair is like saying hello to everybody you see. A few people automatically say 'Hi' right back; most people get furious that you disturbed their environment."

"**Jerry**, *you have so much to offer*. If only you'd cut your hair. People laugh at you. They don't take you seriously."

"Listen, Aunt Sadie, *long hair* is what makes them take us seriously! Wherever we go, our hair tells people

Roz Payne

where we stand on Vietnam, Wallace, campus disruption, dope. We're living TV commercials for the revolution. We're walking picket signs.

"Every response to longhairs creates a moral crisis for straights. We force adults to bring all their repressions to the surface, to expose their real feelings."

"**Feelings**, **schmeelings**, **Jerry**," Aunt Sadie said. "I'm telling you that in my time we were radicals. We were invited to a convention in the Soviet Union to meet Stalin.

And who did they pick to represent us? Who did they pick? I'm telling you who they picked.

"They picked the people who were down-to-earth, who were clean and nice. I didn't have long hair. I didn't smell. . . ."

"Aunt Sadie, I don't want to go to any fucking conventions," I said.

"That doesn't matter," she replied, suddenly pushing aside untasted her bowl full of Nancy's good chicken soup. "But you should be clean and nice. Did your mother teach you to smell bad, maybe?"

"Aunt Sadie, you won't believe this, but you're uptight about your body. Man was born to let his hair grow long and to smell like a man. We are descended from the apes, and we're proud of our ancestry. We're natural men lost in this world of machines and computers. Long hair is more beautiful than short hair. We love our bodies. We even smell our armpits once in a while.

"Grownups used to tell us kids that black people smelled bad. We asked, 'What's wrong with Negroes?' and they said, 'Did you ever get close enough to smell them?' If middle-class people say that now about blacks, they'll get a good black-power punch across their fucking mouths, so they say it about longhairs. We ask them, 'Did you ever get close enough to smell a longhair?' and they shout back at us, 'Go take a bath.'

"Amerikans are puritans. Amerikans are afraid of sex. Amerika creates a sexual prison in which men think they have to be supermen and have to see sensitivity as weakness. Women are taught that self-assertion is unfeminine. *So Marines go to Vietnam and get their asses kicked by Viet Kong women.*

"Long hair is the beginning of our liberation from the sexual oppression that underlies this whole military society. Through long hair we're engaged in a sexual assault that's going to destroy the political-economic structure of Amerikan society!"

"God help you destroy it, **Jerry**," Aunt Sadie wailed, chicken-soup tears dribbling down her cheeks. "But you'd be so much more effective if you would cut your hair and dress nicely."

Aunt Sadie and I weren't getting very far. It was sad that the two black sheep in the family couldn't identify with each other.

"**Jerry**," Aunt Sadie said, getting up to leave. "Just remember one thing: there are two classes in the world, the bourgeoisie and the working class. You're either on one side or the other. It has nothing to do with hair.

"If you'd only get a haircut. You're only hurting yourself. . . ."

I embraced her, took the $20 she gave me to buy "some nice new clothes," and waved good-bye.

"Watch out, Aunt Sadie!" I shouted as she left. *"Some of the most longhaired people I know are bald."*

17: Keep Pot Illegal

Marijuana makes each person God.

Get high and you want to turn on the world. It's never "my dope"—it's always "our dope." Everything for everybody. The Communist drug.

Pot transforms environments. All the barriers we build to protect ourselves from each other disappear.

Grass travels around the room like a continually moving kiss. Smoke grass in the morning. Stay high all day.

The eight-hour day is the enemy.

When you're high on pot you enjoy only one thing—the moment. A minute feels like an hour; an hour can be a minute. *"Damn it, I missed that appointment."* All appointments and schedules, times and deadlines disappear. Man can do what he wants whenever he wants to do it.

Marijuana is the street theater of the mind.

Marijuana is destroying the schools. Education is conditioning. Pot deconditions. School makes us cynics. Pot makes us dreamers.

Education polarizes our brains into subjects, categories, divisions, concepts. Pot scrambles up our brains and presents everything as one perfect mess.

We fall off chairs roaring with laughter when we hear our professors, teachers, experts—the people we're supposed to learn from—discussing us, our culture, grass. We feel like those primitive African tribes must have felt when Margaret Mead came popping in with her pencil and paper.

Hearing someone who has not smoked grass talk about it is like hearing a nun talk about sex.

The only expert is the person who *does it.*

The family that smokes together stays together.

Pot is a magic drug because it can transcend the generation gap. Everyone should try to turn on his parents. Marijuana enables the old to become young again; it breaks down defenses parents have about their past.

But it is the rare parent who will even try it. Parents talk about marijuana the way their parents talked about masturbation. How many thousands of kids have been sent to mental hospitals by their parents because they smoke pot? Schools aren't effective enough as prisons: Once inside a mental hospital there's no way out.

Professors are afraid to go to parties with students because they may be handed a joint. And joints are illegal. If joints are illegal, they might get busted. If they get busted, they lose their jobs. The logic of fear. People who fear have nothing to teach us.

In 1968, marijuana became rampant in the army. In 1969 low morale, even civil disobedience, became rampant in the army.

Why does grass inspire the Viet Kong and kill the fighting spirit of the Amerikan GI? Any pot-smoker can understand it: Marijuana is a truth serum. The Viet Kong are defending their parents, children and homes—their deaths are noble and heroic. The Amerikans are fighting for nothing you can see, feel, touch or believe in. Their deaths are futile and wasted. "Why die on Hamburger Hill?" asks the pot-smoking Amerikan soldier, as he points his gun at the head of the captain who ordered him to take a hill that only the Viet Kong want.

If the Pentagon tries to stop pot in the army, she'll end up destroying her army in the process. But if the army brass leaves grass-smokers alone, army bases will soon be as turned on and uncontrollable as college campuses.

What's going to happen when all those Amerikan GI's come home? "What do you mean, we're old enough to fight and die but not old enough to smoke?"

The New Left said: I protest.
The hippies said: I am.
Grass destroyed the left as a minority movement and created in its place a youth culture.

Grass shows us that our lives, not our consciences, are at stake. As pot-heads we come face-to-face with the real world of cops, jails, courts, trials, undercover narcs, paranoia and the war with our parents.

An entire generation of flower-smokers has been turned into criminals. There are more than 200,000 people now in jail for dope. Every pot-head is in jail as long as one is in jail. The solidarity of saliva.

Grass teaches us disrespect for the law and the courts. Which do you trust: Richard Milhous Nixon or your own sense organs?

We are what we get high on.

Juice-heads drink alone. They get drunk and disgusting. They puke all over themselves. They pass out. Alcohol turns off the senses.

Pot-heads smoke together. We get high and get together. Into ourselves and into each other. How can we make a revolution except together?

Make pot legal, and society will fall apart.
Keep it illegal, and soon there will be revolution.

18: Ho Chi Minh Is a Yippie Agent

"The goal of the revolution is to open all doors and break all locks," I told the Vancouver border guard as he hustled me behind a locked door to see if I was morally fit to get into Canada.

"Do you use drugs?" he asked.

"Sure," I said. I cannot tell a lie.

His pen got a hard-on. He checked the "yes" bracket.

"Which?"

"Coca-cola."

"Do you advocate the overthrow of the Canadian government?"

"No," I said. I was still in the United States, and I don't believe you should advocate the overthrow of any country you're not in. A lot of crazy motherfuckers go around the United States recklessly advocating the overthrow of every government except their own: China, Russia, Cuba, North Vietnam.

Then I got pissed off.

"Drop out!" I shouted at the border guard. "There's no such thing as a border between the United States and Canada. It exists only in your head. Our passports are our bodies, and the earth is round."

I tried to get him to take off his uniform. It was a barrier between us.

"This machine will stop only when people like you lay down your pencils. Come with me to the campuses. We got sex, drugs, riots, freedom."

"I'm only doing my job," he said.

I proved myself morally sound—by lying—and got across the border. I'd been invited to the University of British Columbia as visiting inciter-to-riot. Within two hours I faced 2,000 people. I love a crowd. To our parents crowds bring back memories of Hitler and mass hysteria. To us crowds mean freedom.

I wore my Viet Kong flag amidst cheers and boos. "The ground we're standing on is liberated territory!" I screamed. "Whenever we see a rule, we must break it. Society has turned us into cops, taught us to police ourselves. Only by breaking rules do we discover who we are.

"We got to destroy the universities, tear down this building, break out of jail, write fuck on the walls. School teaches us to be critics of life. Fuck critics. Fuck criticism. Stop being critics and start living.

"Don't sit out there thinking, 'I agree with him on this point and disagree with him on that one.' Fuck whether you *agree* or *disagree* with me. That's an academic bullshit trip. I don't want your agreement or your disagreement. I don't care whether you approve or disapprove. I want *your life*. The revolution wants *your body*."

The crowd was getting warmed up.

"Is there any place on this campus that needs liberating?" I asked.

Someone shouted, "The Faculty Club!"

A few people turned in that direction. Then everybody, all 2,000 people spontaneously started marching toward the club.

We barged right into the exclusive little lounge. The professors freaked out, spilled soup all over their suits and ran for cover. We began liberating the place.

The first thing liberated was the liquor; drinks were passed out free to everybody. Within an hour, grass was being smoked everywhere. Some people were rolling joints in five- and ten-dollar bills.

Some people took off their clothes and jumped into the faculty pool. An Amerikan student climbed to a chair and burned his draft card. Somebody took my Viet Kong flag. Soon it was flying over the building.

TV cameras arrived to interview the liberators.

People kept asking each other, "Why are we doing this?" Nobody understood what he was doing. Fraternity boys, business students, academic types, hippies, radicals, clean faces, shorthairs, longhairs, moustaches. Every campus "type" was there. We had touched a common but nameless emotion.

The head of the Faculty Club, a commerce professor, tried to co-opt the orgy. He stood on top of a chair and thanked everyone for coming. He invited people to stay for the afternoon.

"You never invited us before!" someone shouted. The room responded with catcalls, and the professor lost his temper. "You're stealing the liquor. We could call the police and prosecute. But as long as you don't burn anything, you can stay."

The orgy continued for thirty-six hours. Its impact on Canada was traumatic. The staid Canadian press couldn't understand what had happened; why did usually well-behaved Canadian students spontaneously burst forth in childish rebellion?

"It was really sad," wrote the *Vancouver Province*, "that such a snake-oil vendor as Jerry Rubin could turn some of the students temporarily into uncritical sheep. . . . Most heartening was the reaction of official student leaders who saw Rubin as a showman-seditionist whose arguments about university structure have no validity here."

Don Lewis

Political commentators in Amerika are always looking for the causes behind campus disruptions. They blame the Vietnam war. "As soon as the war is over, the campuses will get back to normal," they think.

The October 24 liberation of the British Columbia Faculty Club reveals the forbidden truth. The act of liberation included no list of "demands." It had no "political" purpose. It was a spontaneous event. The truth was contained in the act.

We are not protesting "issues"; we are protesting Western civilization. We are not hassling over shit so that we can go back to "normal" lives: *our "normal" lives are fucked up!*

The Revolution is nonverbal and knows no confines or borders.

If there had been no Vietnam war, we would have invented one.

If the Vietnam war ends, we'll find another war.

Uncle Ho is a yippie agent.

19: Every Revolutionary
Needs a Color TV

Walter Cronkite is SDS's best organizer. Uncle Walter brings out the map of the U. S. with circles around the campuses that blew up today. The battle reports.

Every kid out there is thinking, "Wow! I wanna see *my* campus on that map!"

Television proves the domino theory: one campus falls and they all fall.

The first "student demonstration" flashed across the TV tubes of the nation as a myth in 1964. That year the first generation being raised from birth on TV was 9, 10 and 11 years old. "First chance I get," they thought, "I wanna do that too."

The first chance they got was when they got to junior high and high school five years later—1969! And that was the year Amerika's junior high and high schools exploded! A government survey shows that three out of every five high schools in the country had "some form of active protest" in 1969.

TV is raising generations of kids who want to grow up and become demonstrators.

Have you ever seen a boring demonstration on TV? Just being on TV makes it exciting. Even picket lines look breathtaking. Television creates myths bigger than reality.

Demonstrations last hours, and most of that time nothing happens. After the demonstration we rush home for the six o'clock news. The drama review. TV packs all the action into two minutes—a commercial for the revolution.

The mere idea of a "story" is revolutionary because a "story" implies disruption of normal life. Every reporter is a dramatist, creating a theater out of life.

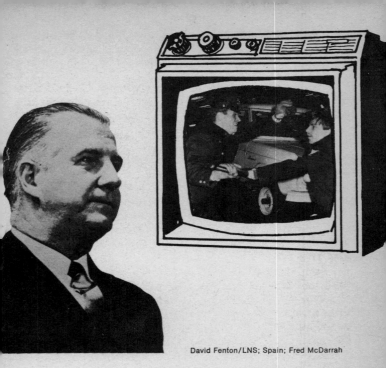

David Fenton/LNS; Spain; Fred McDarrah

Crime in the streets is news; law and order is not. A revolution is news; the status quo ain't.

The media does not *report* "news," it *creates* it. An event *happens* when it goes on TV and becomes myth.

The media is not "neutral." The presence of a camera transforms a demonstration, turning us into heroes. We take more chances when the press is there because we know whatever happens will be known to the entire world within hours.

Television keeps us escalating our tactics; a tactic becomes ineffective when it stops generating gossip or interest—"news."

Politicians get air time just by issuing statements. Rockefeller doesn't have to carry a picket sign to make a point. But ordinary people must take to the streets to get on television. One person, doing the right thing at the right time, can create a myth. The disruption of Nixon's speech reduces Nixon to background.

TV time goes to those with the most guts and imagination.

I never understand the radical who comes on TV in a suit and tie. Turn off the sound and he could be the mayor!

The *words* may be radical, but television is a non-verbal instrument! The way to understand TV is to shut off the sound. No one remembers any words they hear; the mind is a technicolor movie of images, not words.

I've never seen "bad" coverage of a demonstration. It makes no difference what they *say* about us. The pictures are the story.

Our power lies in our ability to strike fear in the enemy's heart: so the more the media exaggerate, the better. When the media start saying nice things about us, we should get worried.

If the yippies controlled national TV, we could make the Viet Kong and the Black Panthers the heroes of swooning Amerikan middle-aged housewives everywhere within a week.

The movement is too puritanical about the use of the media. After all, Karl Marx never watched television!

You can't be a revolutionary today without a television set—it's as important as a gun!

Every guerrilla must know how to use the terrain of the culture that he is trying to destroy!

20 : Fuck God

A dying culture destroys everything it touches.

Language is one of the first things to go.

Nobody really communicates with words anymore. Words have lost their emotional impact, intimacy, ability to shock and make love.

Language *prevents* communication.

> CARS LOVE SHELL
> How can I say
> "I love you"
> after hearing:
> "CARS LOVE SHELL."

Does anyone understand what I *mean*?

Nigger control is called "law and order." Stealing is called "capitalism."

A *"REVOLUTION"* IN TOILET PAPER.

A *"REVOLUTION"* IN COMBATING MOUTH ODOR!

A *"REVOLUTIONARY"* HOLLYWOOD MOVIE!

Have the capitalists no respect?

But there's one word which Amerika hasn't destroyed.

One word which has maintained its emotional power and purity.

Amerika cannot destroy it because she dare not use it.

It's illegal!

It's the last word left in the English language:

FUCK!!!

One bright winter day in Berkeley, John Thomson crayoned on a piece of cardboard "FUCK WAR," sat down with it and was arrested within two minutes. Two more people sat down with signs saying "FUCK WAR." *They* were arrested.

The Filthy Speech Movement had been born.

Everyone at school plays with himself verbally. The Free Speech Movement ended our virginity—we challenged outside society and the cops came on campus to get us. But once they left, everybody went back to playing with himself.

Once you've had sex, jacking off is a drag. Campus sexual frustration led John to start the Filthy Speech Movement.

"Nobody would have gotten excited if I held a sign which said 'Kill Vietnamese,' " John said.

So he said "FUCK WAR" and four mighty letters brought the Great University to a Grinding Halt.

Old people everywhere freaked out. *"Fuck, man, is this what Free Speech is coming to?"* Fucking Clark Kerr the fucking president of the fucking university fucking resigned. He said the fucking future of the whole motherfucking university was at stake. Fuck him, he's a fucking asshole. He said that if FUCK wasn't fucking banished from the minds and mouths of the fucking students, then things were gonna get pretty fucked up.

But most political radicals got uptight and wouldn't defend FUCK. Activists in the Free Speech Movement ostracized the FUCK-heads—they said FUCK wasn't "serious"! They got a sudden pure speech fetish.

Things *did* get fucked-up. In a unity move, Clark Kerr came back and fucked the fuck students. They were expelled from the university and given jail terms. Few politicos gave a fuck.

The Free Speech Movement was raped in the same bed with the Filthy Speech Movement. The movement was badly divided. It was an early sign of the split between political radicals and the hippie/yippies.

How can you separate politics from sex? It's all the same thing: Body politic.

POLITICO-SEXUAL REALITY: The naked human body is immoral under Christianity and illegal under Amerikan law. Nudity is called "indecent exposure." Fuck is a dirty word because you have to be naked to do it. Also it's fun.

When we start playing with our "private parts," our parents say "Don't do that." The mother commits a crime against her child when she says "Don't do that."

We're taught that our shit stinks. We're taught to be ashamed of how we came into the world—fucking. We're taught that if we dig balling, we should feel guilty.

We're taught: body pleasure is immoral!

We're really taught to hate ourselves!

Puritanism leads us to Vietnam. Sexual insecurity results in a supermasculinity trip called imperialism. Amerikan foreign policy especially in Vietnam, makes no sense except sexually. Amerika has a frustrated penis, trying to drive itself into Vietnam's tiny slit to prove it is The Man.

The revolution declares war on Original Sin, the dictatorship of parents over their kids, Christian morality, capitalism and supermasculinity trips.

The yippie political strategy is to ally with Billy Graham. Keep the word "fuck" dirty! At the same time we yippies fight for the right to say fuck whenever we want to. It's a contradiction—but in contradictions like this lie the genius of making a revolution.

Our tactic is to send niggers and longhair scum invading white middle-class homes, fucking on the living room floor, crashing on the chandeliers, spewing sperm on the Jesus pictures, breaking the furniture and smashing Sunday school napalm-blood Amerika forever.

111

We will do whatever is forbidden.

We will outrage Amerika until the bourgeoisie dies of apoplexy.

We will turn Amerika's colleges into nudist camps.

We will find new ways of living together and raising our kids.

FUCKFUCKFUCKFUCKFUCKFUCKFUCKFUCKFUCKFUCKFUCKFUCKFUCK
FUCKFUCKFUCKFUCKFUCKFUCKFUCKFUCKFUCKFUCKFUCKFUCKFUCK
FUCKFUCKFUCKFUCKFUCKFUCKFUCKFUCKFUCKFUCKFUCKFUCKFUCK
FUCKFUCKFUCKFUCKFUCKFUCKFUCKFUCKFUCKFUCKFUCKFUCKFUCK
FUCKFUCKFUCKFUCKFUCKFUCKFUCKFUCKFUCKFUCKFUCKFUCKFUCK
FUCKFUCKFUCKFUCKFUCKFUCKFUCKFUCKFUCKFUCKFUCKFUCKFUCK
FUCKFUCKFUCKFUCKFUCKFUCKFUCKFUCKFUCKFUCKFUCKFUCKFUCK
FUCKFUCKFUCKFUCKFUCKFUCKFUCKFUCKFUCKFUCKFUCKFUCKFUCK
FUCKFUCKFUCKFUCKFUCKFUCKFUCKFUCKFUCKFUCKFUCKFUCKFUCK
FUCKFUCKFUCKFUCKFUCKFUCKFUCKFUCKFUCKFUCKFUCKFUCKFUCK
FUCKFUCKFUCKFUCKFUCKFUCKFUCKFUCKFUCKFUCKFUCKFUCKFUCK
FUCKFUCKFUCKFUCKFUCKFUCKFUCKFUCKFUCKFUCKFUCKFUCKFUCK
FUCKFUCKFUCKFUCKFUCKFUCKFUCKFUCKFUCKFUCKFUCKFUCKFUCK
FUCKFUCKFUCKFUCKFUCKFUCKFUCKFUCKFUCKFUCKFUCKFUCKFUCK
FUCKFUCKFUCKFUCKFUCKFUCKFUCKFUCKFUCKFUCKFUCKFUCKFUCK
FUCKFUCKFUCKFUCKFUCKFUCKFUCKFUCKFUCKFUCKFUCKFUCKFUCK
FUCKFUCKFUCKFUCKFUCKFUCKFUCKFUCKFUCKFUCKFUCKFUCKFUCK
FUCKFUCKFUCKFUCKFUCKFUCKFUCKFUCKFUCKFUCKFUCKFUCKFUCK
FUCKFUCKFUCKFUCKFUCKFUCKFUCKFUCKFUCKFUCKFUCKFUCKFUCK
FUCKFUCKFUCKFUCKFUCKFUCKFUCKFUCKFUCKFUCKFUCKFUCKFUCK
FUCKFUCKFUCKFUCKFUCKFUCKFUCKFUCKFUCKFUCKFUCKFUCKFUCK
FUCKFUCKFUCKFUCKFUCKFUCKFUCKFUCKFUCKFUCKFUCKFUCKFUCK
FUCKFUCKFUCKFUCKFUCKFUCKFUCKFUCKFUCKFUCKFUCKFUCKFUCK
FUCKFUCKFUCKFUCKFUCKFUCKFUCKFUCKFUCKFUCKFUCKFUCKFUCK
FUCKFUCKFUCKFUCKFUCKFUCKFUCKFUCKFUCKFUCKFUCKFUCKFUCK
FUCKFUCKFUCKFUCKFUCKFUCKFUCKFUCKFUCKFUCKFUCKFUCKFUCK
FUCKFUCKFUCKFUCKFUCKFUCKFUCKFUCKFUCKFUCKFUCKFUCKFUCK
FUCKFUCKFUCKFUCKFUCKFUCKFUCKFUCKFUCKFUCKFUCKFUCKFUCK
FUCKFUCKFUCKFUCKFUCKFUCKFUCKFUCKFUCKFUCKFUCKFUCKFUCK
FUCKFUCKFUCKFUCKFUCKFUCKFUCKFUCKFUCKFUCKFUCKFUCKFUCK
FUCKFUCKFUCKFUCKFUCKFUCKFUCKFUCKFUCKFUCKFUCKFUCKFUCK

21 : Ideology Is a Brain Disease

The revolution is *now*. We create the revolution by *living* it.

What would happen if the white ideological left group took power: Communist Party, Trotskyites, Progressive Labor, Independent Socialists, Outer Mongolian Proletarian Internationalists and the rest of the alphabet soup?

The hippie streets would be the first cleaned up by "socialist" pigs. We'd be forced to get haircuts and shaves every week. We'd have to bathe every night, and we'd go to jail for saying dirty words.

Sex, except to produce children for the revolution, would be illegal.

Psychedelic drugs would be capital crimes and beer-drinking mandatory.

We'd have to attend compulsory political-education classes at least five nights a week.

Rock dancing would be taboo, and miniskirts, Hollywood movies and comic books illegal.

The left says to the yippies, "You're not serious."

They tell us only the "working class" can make the revolution as they walk into the university libraries carrying *The New York Times* and *The New Republic*. Would a university radical be caught dead watching TV, reading the *New York Daily News* or digging a baseball game? The left is waiting for the workers to come to the university.

The yippies will consider the left serious when it starts printing comic books. We gotta reduce politics to the simplicity of a rock 'n' roll lyric.

The left would rather hand a soldier a leaflet than a joint.

The left turns Communism into a church with priests defining "the line." It's a Christian trip all the way. Study

YIP-OUT: RESURRECTION OF FREE
CENTRAL PARK/ALL DAY/EASTER SUNDAY

Martin Carey

and sacrifice to make the revolution. Suffering will free you and the working class.

The ideological left is made up of part-time people whose life-style mocks their rhetoric. There's a thousand miles between their actions and their ideology. How can you be a revolutionary going to school during the day and attending meetings at night? How can you be a part-time person in a full-time revolution?

114

"DROP OUT!" the yippies scream at them. *Revolution is not what you believe, what organization you belong to, or who you vote for—it's what you do all day, how you live.*

The left drives people away almost as fast as Nixon drives people toward us. (Thank God Nixon does a better job!) Ideological hassles on theoretical bullshit, boring meetings—is this the life of a revolutionary? Who's going to give his life to a movement with that kind of come-on?

Yippies scream: "You don't know what you're missing if you're not in the revolution! *Yippie!*" The romance of our revolutionary life-style, freedom and fighting will draw the children of the working class to the revolution.

Many intellectual radicals arrogantly call themselves "Marxists." (Poor Karl.) They're very mechanical, telling us the "Laws of Marxism" say revolution comes *only* out of economic exploitation. There'll be revolution *only* if there's another economic depression.

Their theories don't explain us—a revolutionary movement that has come out of affluence, not poverty. We don't fit into any of their preconceived "scientific" categories. They say the only role for whites is to "support"—support the Black Panthers, support the "working class," support the Chinese.

The yippies see white middle-class youth as a revolutionary class. We are exploited and oppressed, and we are fighting for *our freedom*. We do not feel *guilty* because we're not black, Chinese or factory workers. Capitalism will die because it cannot satisfy its own children!

But then the liberal intellectuals tell us that a revolution has never taken place in an industrialized affluent country. Nothing in history has ever happened till it happens!

Get out of your universities, leftists!
Watch TV!
Turn on! Drop out!
Get high!
Act!

Culver Pictures, Inc.

Act first. Analyze later. Impulse—not theory—makes the great leaps forward. Theory comes when people try to figure out what they did—*after* they do it. Mao says: "We learn *most* from our *mistakes*."

For years I went to left-wing meetings trying to figure out what the hell was going on. Finally I started taking acid, and I realized what was going on: nothing. I vowed never to go to another left-wing meeting again. Fuck left-wing meetings!

None of the movement's great historical events—from the Be-in to the Pentagon to Chicago—came out of a left-wing meeting. In fact, they would all have been voted down!

The yippies are Marxists. We follow in the revolutionary tradition of Groucho, Chico, Harpo and Karl.

What the yippies learn from Karl Marx—history's most infamous, bearded, longhaired, hippie commie freek agitator—is that we must create a spectacular myth of revolution.

Karl wrote and sang his own rock album called "The Communist Manifesto."

"The Communist Manifesto" is a song that has overthrown governments.

116

22: Money Is Shit—Burning Money, Looting and Shoplifting Can Get You High

The Stock Exchange official looks worried. He says to us, "You can't see the Stock Exchange."

We're aghast. "Why not?" we ask.

"Because you're hippies and you've come to demonstrate."

"Hippies?" Abbie shouts, outraged at the very suggestion. "We're Jews and we've come to see the stock market."

VISION: *The next day's headlines*:
NEW YORK STOCK MARKET BARS JEWS.

We've thrown the official a verbal karate punch. He relents.

The stock market comes to a complete standstill at our entrance at the top of the balcony. The thousands of brokers stop playing Monopoly and applaud us. What a crazy sight for them—longhaired hippies staring down at them.

We throw dollar bills over the ledge. Floating currency fills the air. Like wild animals, the stockbrokers climb all over each other to grab the money.

"This is what it's all about, real live money!!! Real dollar bills! People are starving in Biafra!" we shout.

We introduce a little reality into their fantasy lives.

While throwing the money we spot the cops coming. The cops grab us and throw us off the ledge and into the elevators. The stockbrokers below loudly boo the pigs.

We find ourselves in front of the stock market at high noon. The strangest creeps you ever saw are walking around

117

us: people with short hair, long ties, business suits and brief cases.

They're so serious.

We start dancing "Ring Around the Rosey" in front of the Stock Exchange.

And then we begin burning the things they worship: dollar bills!

Straight people start yelling: "Don't! Don't do that!"

One man rushes to get a burning $5 bill out of Abbie's hand, but it's too late. The money is *poof!*

A crowd assembles; emotions are high. The police come to break it up. We split into the subway.

Three weeks later *The New York Times* reports: "The New York Stock Exchange last night installed bullet-proof glass panels and a metal grillwork ceiling on its visitors' gallery for what an exchange spokesman said were 'reasons of security.'

"Last August 24 a dozen or so hippies threw dollar bills from the gallery—a display many exchange members do not want to see repeated."

* * *

The Great Socialist Debate Hall is decorated with personality posters of Trotsky, Malcolm X and Che on the wall. I was invited to debate 200-pound Fred Halstead, the Socialist Workers Party's 1968 candidate for president of the United States. The subject: "What Policy Next for the Anti-War Movement?"

I arrived at the debate with bodyguards, Keith and Judy Lampe, at my side. Keith wore an English bobbie's uniform and Judy was a pregnant CIA agent with high-collared trench coat and large hat; she held a blowtorch.

"I got a number of death threats before the meeting," I explained to the crowd of four hundred people.

These far-left ideological groups try to make us think their debates are of historical significance. Everyone in the audience must stay in his seat just as if he's in class. Each debater has 30 minutes to speak, then 10 minutes for rebuttal. Then a young Trot flunkie goes through the audience selling *Militants* and waking everybody up for the question period. Finally the masterdebaters give three-minute conclusions.

Truth wins out in the end.

My turn. On a portable phonograph I played Dylan and the Beatles. "Something Is Happening But You Don't Know What It Is, Do You, Mr. Jones?" and "I Am a Walrus."

"Stupid schmuck," a woman shouted. "He's not saying a word."

119

It was the first time in the history of the Socialist movement that someone didn't say a word during the time allotted for political argument.

I burned my draft card. The room became a carnival. Everyone talked at once. The music released inhibitions. Then I burned a dollar bill.

"Why don't you give that dollar to people who are poor and who need it?" a "Socialist" called out.

I was shocked. The "Socialists" see money just like the capitalists do. As a real thing.

"How can you burn money when poor people in the ghetto need it?" another "Socialist" asked.

I smiled and burned another piece of green paper. Around the room shorthaired socialists hissed and booed the burning of money.

"You should join the circus!" they cried.

Yippies all around the room stood and burned bills.

Money is a drug. Amerika is a drug culture, a nation of crazy addicts. Money can be used for cigarette paper. Roll a joint. Smoke it.

"What do you do?"

That means: "How do you make your money?" Your work is that thing which produces your money. It defines who you are. Our very consciousness is warped by the green fetish!

Money causes the separation between work and life. People don't do what they dig because they want smelly money. People don't dig what they do because they work for the dollar.

No artist ever did it for the bread. If money motivates you, you're not an artist.

People see each other not as human beings, but as financial transactions. The medium is the message. Money corrupts every human relationship it touches.

Fidel Castro says: "We've done away with a lot of privileges and inequalities and we want all of them to disappear, but the real problem isn't to redistribute income or

121

equalize wages. We must break from the mastery of money, get rid of money altogether. We're not out to manage the old system more efficiently."

Since money is the standard for the system, people judge themselves and their work financially. People consider their lives won or lost by their collection of fiscal feces.

Liberation comes when we stop doing it for the bread and do what we always wanted to do as children.

(If the Beatles listened to their own music, they would burn all their money.)

The money-economy is immoral, based totally on power and manipulation, offending the natural exchange between human beings: an exchange based on common need. Looting is a natural expression of the money system. Capitalism is stealing. A system based on stealing can never condemn stealing. Everything should be free for all if it is free for some.

(Bonnie Parker and Clyde Barrow are the leaders of the New Youth.)

All money represents theft. To steal from the rich is a sacred and religious act. To take what you need is an act of self-love, self-liberation. While looting, a man to his own self is true.

(Shoplifting gets you high. Don't buy. Steal. If you act like it's yours, no one will ask you to pay for it.)

Schools and churches are pushovers when up against money. Schools have no soul because they know where they get their bread. Churches dig profit. In church an exploiter can feel at home and fancy himself in heaven.

(To panhandle man-to-man on the street in this country is a noble, liberating act. What's a college president if not an uptight panhandler?)

Money is violence. Money is not so dramatic a killer as napalm, but Amerika kills far more people with her dollar than she does with her bombs. Instead of U.S.-Latin American export-import statistics, read "infant deaths, human beings exploited and sacrificed, dignity denied."

(Money is the way whites hope to continue to control blacks. Smell money and smell the desire for control.)

Money is the bond between parents and children, holding the family together, but really ripping it apart. Money introduces pride, guilt, debt, obligation, responsibility.

(Kids should steal money from their parents, because that is true liberation from the money ethic: true family.)

Money means: Work today so you can enjoy "tomorrow." Which never comes. Money causes unnecessary discipline, boredom, suffering, pain.

Amerika will become free only when the dollar bill becomes worthless.

A society which makes eating a privilege, not a right, has no right to exist.

(𝔈at your money and die.)

Burning money (*and credit cards and banks and property*) is an act of love, an act on behalf of humanity.

PAY
TOILET
EACH 5¢ PATRON
INSERT
ONE NICKEL
IN SLOT
TURN KNOB AND
PULL

23: I Agree With Your Tactics, I Don't Know About Your Goals

Give us an inch—we'll take a mile.

Satisfy our demands, and we got twelve more. The more demands you satisfy, the more we got.

I never know what the "issues" are at demonstrations. They're always decided by people who like to go to meetings to debate for hours what the issues should be.

All we want from those meetings are demands that the Establishment can never satisfy. What a defeat if they satisfy our demands!

Demonstrators are never "reasonable." We always put our demands forward in such an obnoxious manner that the power structure can never satisfy us and remain the power structure. Then, we scream, righteously angry, when our demands are not met.

Satisfy our demands and we lose.

Deny our demands and through struggle we achieve the love and brotherhood of a community.

People who say: "I agree with your goals, but I don't know about your tactics," smell of foul horseshit. Goals are irrelevant. The tactics, the actions, are critical.

If we had to decide beforehand what our goals would be, we'd be arguing about the future society for the next 1,000 years. Let's worry about that bridge when we come to it. *The goal now is to blow up the bridge just behind us.*

Do. Do. Do. The movement gets its unity around tactics. We become a community through collective action.

People are always asking us, "What's your program?" I hand them a Mets scorecard. Or I tell them to check the yellow pages. "Our program's there." *Fuck programs!* The goal of revolution is to abolish programs and turn specta-

Mel Zimmer

tors into actors. It's a do-it-yourself revolution, and we'll work out the future as we go.

Castro says: "The goal of the Cuban revolution is to turn *every* individual into a legislator."

Representative democracy is the enemy. The goal is each-man-his-own-revolution.

Walk on red lights.

Don't walk on green lights.

Try to give away nickels and dimes to people on the street. "Do you need some money free?" Watch how frightened people are to take anything—even money—*free!*

If you walk down the street and see someone you want to kiss, do it. *Kiss!*

Go into a bank, business or office and demand to use the toilet. You'll be told, "No *public* bathroom here." Stand on one leg and whine loudly, "I gotta doo-doo."

Tell them that if they continue to refuse, you'll shit on the floor.

Shit on the floor!

Nancy, Peter Rabbit and I were kicked out of the Newport Folk Festival for giving pornographic literature to a nun: the leaflet said, "Fuck the first nun you see."

Call up a telephone operator and ask her for a date, ask her what's her favorite color, talk to her as a human being, not as a phone operator.

Go on airplanes humming the "Internationale" and carrying a guitar case and a Spanish dictionary. The dream of every airline stewardess is to get hijacked.

When you're going through the toll booth on a freeway, pay the toll for a few cars behind you.

Or better yet: Dynamite the toll booths, because they charge money for people to get across free land.

Blow up Howard Johnson's on the turnpike—the universal oppressor of everybody.

126

When in doubt, burn. Fire is the revolutionary's god. Fire is instant theater. No words can match fire.

Politicians only notice poverty when the ghettos burn.

The burning of the first draft card caused earth tremors under the Pentagon.

Burn the flag. Burn churches.

Burn, burn, burn.

There's no such thing as a bad tactic. Put down nothing. The John Birch Society shows how effective even letter-writing can be. I know a woman in Iowa who wears a black armband everywhere she goes, even into the shower.

Alienate.
Alienate.
Alienate.

The more people you alienate, the more people you reach. If you don't alienate people, you're not reaching them.

When planning a demonstration, always include a role for the cops. Most people don't get excited until the cops come in. Nothing radicalizes like a cop. Cops are perfectly dressed for the role of "bad guy."

The basic issue in Amerika today is clothes. The Marx Brothers are our leaders as they run through restaurants cutting off people's ties. Suits and ties will be illegal in the Communist society; the suit-and-tie is the manifestation of class snobbery.

Amerika puts her people into prisons by carefully defining their roles. How do you know what a man's role is? By his clothes. All you need for a job in Amerika is the clothes.

Want to be a lawyer? Get yourself a blue suit, a couple of yellow legal pads, a briefcase and a client. Go to court next week and identify yourself as a lawyer. Start entering motions, writs, pleas for abatements, petitions, beseechments and anything else you can think of. Nobody will ever ask you for your law degree.

A judge puts on his robe and suddenly be becomes a Big Motherfucker. Takes off his robe and he's like any other schmuck on the street.

Want to be a nun? Get into the habit.

Become an impostor. The yippies try to liberate people by getting everybody to change their clothes. As a transitional stage towards Communism, the yippies demand that everybody change his job and his clothes every few months. Everybody should interchange roles with others so that we can all share our experiences.

Communist society will usher in Universal Man. The economy will be a game of musical chairs. Everybody will drive a cab, sell shoes, grow food on a farm, work on a newspaper. The expert-specialist will be a museum piece.

Society will have traveled full circle, from nonspecialization through industrialization and specialization, back to automation and nonspecialization.

Turn every event into historic and mythic significance. Make yourself a symbol.

The revolution is a battle between symbols. Fuck, what's Vietnam anyway? The United States doesn't give a shit about that little piece of real estate. Vietnam is a symbol. The Viet Kong are in San Diego.

If the Viet Kong win, it will inspire free men everywhere: The United States is a paper tiger! If the United States can stop the Viet Kong, then it will inspire pigs everywhere.

Cops enter an occupied university building to arrest students:

"You're under arrest for trespassing."

"We're not trespassing; we're overthrowing the government."

"I don't care what you're doing. You're under arrest for trespassing."

It's hard to see yourself as Che Guevara when society tells you that you're "trespassing."

Amerika tries to take the symbolic meaning out of our actions. Look at the criminal record of a political activist. It reads like the record of a sex deviant—public nuisance, loitering, disorderly conduct, trespassing, disturbing the peace.

I was arrested in Chicago on a sex charge—for "solicitation to commit mob action."

Amerikan youth is looking for a reason to die. A reason to die is a reason to live. Amerika gives us no reason to die—or live.

Wide World Photos, Inc.

The only people in the world today who give our lives meaning are revolutionaries fighting for their freedom.

If Richard Nixon hates the Viet Kong so much, why doesn't he volunteer to go to the front lines himself, instead of sending other parents' sons to die?

Jack Kennedy sent Cuban exiles and Amerikan soldiers to "liberate" Cuba in 1961. Fidel leaped into a tank and went right to the battle zone. If anybody was going to die defending Cuba, it was going to be Fidel himself.

Che did not sign a bureaucratic memo in an air-conditioned office ordering others to fight in Bolivia; he went right to Bolivia and put *his* own life on the line.

Che is a bigger hero to Amerikan youth than Jack or Bobby Kennedy. The Kennedys live on in memorial libraries, but their myths died with their bodies. Che lives on— in each one of us. You gotta be born a Kennedy. Anybody can become a Che. Revolutionaries have eternal life—because we live on in each other.

Even Hollywood is hip to that. Hollywood cranked out a bullshit movie called "Che." Can you imagine Hollywood making a movie called "Dick"—the life of Richard Nixon? What would happen in the movie? A musical: Nixon directing the government like Lawrence Welk and his champagne music.

Do you know any kid in the world who wants to grow up and be like Richard M. Nixon?

We yippies are cocky because we know HISTORY WILL ABSOLVE US.

The history books will see us—the freeks, not the straights—as the heroes of the 1970's.

We know that because we are going to write the history books.

24: *Revolution Is Theater-in-the-Streets*

Al Copeland

You are the stage.
You are the actor.
Everything is for real.
There is no audience.

The goal is to turn on everybody who can be turned on and turn off everybody else.

Theater has no rules, forms, structures, standards, traditions—it is pure, natural energy, impulse, anarchy.

The job of the revolution is to smash stage sets, start fires in movie theaters and then scream, "Fire!"

The theatrical geniuses of today are creating the drama of Vietnam in occupied school administration buildings across Amerika.

The Living Theater, a far-out guerrilla theater group, came to Berkeley while people were fighting the National Guard in the streets. As pacifists they opposed the street action.

Living Theater eliminated the stage and joined the audience. Revolutionary theater.

"I am not allowed to smoke marijuana," one Living Theater member sobbed. He was offered five joints.

Another cried, "I can't take off my clothes!" Around him people stripped naked.

At the end of the performance, everyone left to take the revolution to the streets. The cast stopped at the front door.

Revolution-in-the-auditorium is a contradiction. We get pissed when our revolutionary energy is wasted with a play that is defined by walls and exit doors, by starting and ending times, by ticket prices.

The only role of theater is to take people out of the auditorium and into the streets. The role of the revolutionary theater group is to make the revolution.

*   *   *

The college newspaper editors had this superconference in Washington, D.C., late in 1967. They invited a token yippie. But there is no such thing as a *token* yippie. Where one yippie goes, all yippies go. Ask for one and get a thousand.

So we went to Washington to meet the college editors.

We freaked out as soon as we arrived. The editors were all alike. Carbon copies of each other. Is there a factory somewhere producing college editors? They conversed as if they were talking to each other on the telephone. There they were, person-to-person, in the swank Sheraton-Park Hotel in Washington, D.C., and they had long-distance, talking-on-the-telephone conversations and personalities.

Their campuses had been burning down all year, and they were hung up about whether they would compromise their journalistic "integrity" by editorializing on the Vietnam war.

Just keeping quiet amidst all the bullshit was a cop-out, I felt. It implied the discussion was "reasonable." Is the Vietnam war merely a subject for disagreement between reasonable men? Do these editors think a hassle between a Southern redneck cop's club and a black man's head is only a difference of opinion between two reasonable men?

Paul Krassner, tripping on acid, got so hysterical over their matter-of-factness that he began to bawl. "People are dying in Vietnam, and you're talking like this," he sobbed over and over.

The boy editors did not understand just how conspiratorial we yippies are. We infiltrated their program committee to set up a rigged debate for the afternoon: "Should College Newspaper Editors Association Take a Stand on the War?" That morning we all dropped acid and got ready for battle.

Dig this: Some of the editor-looking people in suits, short hair and ties at the debate were members of the Washington Street Theater. Only 15 of the 500 "editors" were consciously actors, but I couldn't tell who was who. I couldn't believe anybody was a real editor. Everybody acted like an actor. Everybody was playing "editor." Who was real; who was unreal?

It was the most stupid discussion I'd ever heard: Should we take a stand standing up? Sitting down? On the toilet? For negotiations? For the war? Against the war? Has the Associated Press taken a stand on the war? Who is the Associated Press?

Someone made a motion to table all resolutions and take no stand. The motion passed. Suddenly the lights

went out and across the wall flashed scenes of World War II fighting, burning Vietnamese villages, crying Vietnamese women and napalmed children, image after image. The room echoed with hysterical screams. *"Stop it! Stop it! Stop it!"*

A voice boomed over a bullhorn: "Attention! This is Sergeant Haggerty of the Washington Police. These films were smuggled illegally into the country from North Vietnam. We have confiscated them and arrested the people who are responsible. Now clear this room! Anyone still here in two minutes will be arrested!"

The editors fell over themselves rushing for the door. People were trampled. Noses bloodied. Clothes ripped to shreds. They believed they were going to be arrested for seeing a fucking film. They believe they live in a Nazi country. They accept it.

A husky crewcut cat, in suit-and-tie with a name tag saying he was an editor from Brigham Young University, climbed up on a chair and yelled, "I've just come back from Vietnam. My brothers have died in my arms. The fools in the White House are going to kill us all. We are college editors. We have power. We must be brave!"

Is this guy real? Or part of the Washington Theater group? I didn't know. But did it make any difference? Everything was *real* and *unreal*.

The editors were stunned. Chaos and anarchy reigned. The longhaired college editor who had plotted with the yippies freaked out at the monster he had created. "You will have to decide for yourself whether the police are real or not."

"We have been taken for fools," an editor from Duke blurted out. People broke down, crying. They began talking to one another off the telephone. It was an emotional breakthrough.

Through theater they learned something about themselves.

135

Up against yourselves, motherfuckers.

Senator Eugene McCarthy was coming to a press conference later that afternoon. The college editors were going to run a real "Meet the Press" show. They pleaded with us not to disrupt it.

"Bullshit," I thought. Showbiz is showbiz. A press conference is free theater for anyone who can make the best use of it.

The purpose of a press conference is to make news. News is free. Why assume that the only one who can make news is the candidate who answers questions?

Somebody nearby was reading a *New York Post*, and I saw headlines: REDS CRACK HUE JAIL, FREE 2000. *A delirious rush!* Two thousand human beings who were in jail just hours ago were now free! McCarthy claimed to be against the war. For what other reason could he be against the war except to see the Viet Kong free?

McCarthy, distinguished, reserved and gray, finished his 15-minute speech and was clearing his throat to answer questions when I jumped on the stage, put my arm around his shoulder and shouted joyously: "Gene, people are free! People are free in Vietnam today! Aren't you happy?"

The television cameras were grinding away. I wanted to kiss McCarthy, but he was too cold, too unresponsive. I felt like an unrequited lover, my emotion unreturned. Gene tried to ignore me, continuing the press conference as if I weren't there.

Within seconds five more yippies on all fours, yipping like little puppies, were snapping at his heels.

The editors freaked out. They begged us to stop. Gene was surrounded by the revolutionary Marx Brothers. We made faces at him. We cheered. We booed. But he went on, trying to defuse this crisis just as he wanted to defuse the Vietnam crisis with cop-out liberal bullshit.

An Indian drum in the background. Dum-dum-da-dum. Ten people ominously carried a coffin toward us, slowly as in a funeral procession. As they got closer and closer, Gene got edgier and edgier.

"Don't worry, Gene," I said. But he was still trying to pretend I wasn't there.

The coffin carriers approached McCarthy. The coffin had a sign which said, "Electoral Politics." They overturned the coffin and hundreds of McCarthy buttons tumbled out with a crumpled Amerikan flag. McCarthy turned away and split from the press conference.

The college editors were uptight, very uptight. They started moving toward me, hungry for blood. They seethed with stronger emotions than they had over Vietnam. Their professional reputations had been spoiled. They went berserk.

"What are you so pissed off about?" I asked. "McCarthy paid us $20 to do this. His campaign was dull. He did it to make national television."

Up on the wall went signed resignations of embarrassed editors. One editor tried to punch out a yippie.

Being an ex-reporter, I felt self-righteous. "We gave you a story, and you're angry! Are you trying to be reporters like your daddies? Fuck press conferences.

"Go home and watch television!" I screamed. "TV is putting you all out of business!"

*   *   *

Straight people expect radicals to march in circles, carry picket signs and shout slogans. Radicals have to put away their picket signs and start using their wits.

Dig it: Bobby Kennedy was coming to San Francisco to speak at a $500 a plate dinner for Big Democrats.

$500-a-Plate!!!

Some people must be awful hungry!

What do Democrats do, fast for weeks so they can come on like starving lions, devouring fantastic quantities of food, refilling their plates time and time again, and finally ending up in a lusty chorus of belches: "Now that was a damn good $500-dinner, Bobby"?

It sounded like a rotten deal to us, paying $500 for dinner. Some of us don't see $500 in a year's time. So we got to Kennedy's dinner an hour early and set up a table outside with bread, bologna and mustard, and we made lots of bologna sandwiches to give free to all the necklaced women and tailcoated men coming to eat Senator Kennedy's big dinner.

When the straight people arrived, us freeks shouted to them, "Have a free bologna sandwich! Why pay $500 for bologna inside when you can get free bologna right here?"

"You scum, you dirt, you filth!" they screamed back at us.

I thought only Republicans talked like that.

We were even prepared for the Jack Newfield-types, liberal fuck-offs who come on to revolutionaries real chummy-chum-chum.

"We're really for Castro," they explained, "but we're working for Kennedy so that we can make things easier for revolutionaries. Besides we got free tickets."

We made the phony liberals prove their friendship to us by eating our bologna sandwiches. Those bologna sandwiches were guaranteed to ruin their appetites. Then they wouldn't dig Bobby's $500 dinner.

You are what you eat!

*   *   *

Suppose one day 5,000 trucks traveled through a city announcing, "The war in Vietnam is over! The war is over! Turn on your radio for further information." Within two minutes everybody would be calling their mothers. "Hey, Mom. The war's over!" Nixon would have to go on TV to reassure the Amerikan people that the war was still *on*.

We plastered World War II vintage posters of a sailor kissing his girl on V-D day all over New York City. They announced the celebration of the end of the Vietnam War.

Two thousand teenagers and assorted nuts showed up at Washington Square Park.

We didn't know what to do with ourselves, so we went around playing with our noisemakers and telling each other, "The war is over!" (For most of us, the war had never begun.)

Then we got into a huge huddle and started counting backwards—100, 99, 98, 97, 96—and as we got into the 20's more freeks joined in and when we hit 1, everybody screamed, "The war is over!" and we ran up Fifth Avenue to share the good news with fellow Amerikans.

We caught the cops unprepared. They thought we were going to be nice boys and girls and celebrate the end of the war by playing in the park sandbox all afternoon.

But instead we surged through the streets screaming, "The war is over!" Cab drivers honked their horns. People abandoned their cars to come ask us, "What did you say?" Even prowar types said, "Is it really? How do you know?" Allen Ginsberg ran into Automats, threw his hands to the sky, leaped into the air and shouted at the top of his lungs, "The war's over! The war's over!"

Everything was part of the celebration. New York cops on horses and in squad cars with sirens screaming came to clear the streets. We thought the police were celebrating the end of the war, too: they brought their own noisemakers and props. Red and green lights, animals, traffic jams and noise all became part of the celebration.

Nobody was sorry to hear the war was over. And even more amazing, nobody asked, "Who won?"

Nobody gave a fuck.

The celebration broke people out of their accustomed roles. Prowar people couldn't figure out how to react to this psychological assault on their minds. They couldn't ignore it like they could have ignored signs saying, "End the war."

Because theater grows out of each situation, the key to theater is timing. In the summer of '67 it was appropriate to shout that the war was over. But then LBJ pulled a theatrical trick on us: *he* said the war *is* over.

The role of the Peace Movement during the Paris negotiations is to show people that the war is still *on.*

The yippie demonstration in Chicago was the reverse of the War Is Over celebration. We ran through the streets shouting, "The war is on!"

It was.

*   *   *

The CIA is conducting an exhaustive dragnet to find the teenagers who call themselves the Crazies, and who have struck terror throughout the city of New York, invading public meetings at peak moments, ripping off all their clothes, shouting "Rome Wasn't Destroyed in a Day!" and then disappearing mysteriously into the night.

They dressed as waiters at a big feast of liberal senators at the Hilton. J. William Fulbright, J. Kenneth Galbraith and Ed Muskie, expecting their dessert of apple pie and coffee, instead were served pigs' heads on platters.

Then Robin and Sharon stripped and stood radiantly naked before the thousands of middle-class people. Horrified women hid their eyes. Men giggled and stared. Shelley Winters threw her cocktail at them.

Some women began beating naked Crazie Sharon's beautiful thighs with umbrellas.

One woman shouted: **"BEAT HER! SHE'S NAKED!"**

And all across the room liberals shouted, **"BEAT HER, SHE'S NAKED!"**

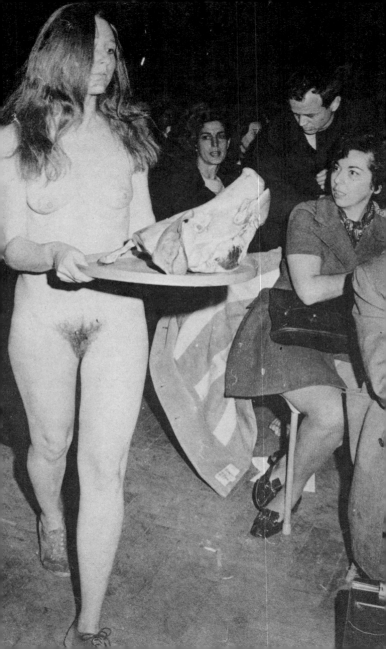

The power structure automatically imposes a frame of reference which forces people to see things from the Man's point of view. When a policeman shoots a nigger, that's "law and order." But when a black man defends himself against a pig, that's "violence."

The role of the revolutionary is to create theater which creates a revolutionary frame of reference. The power to define is the power to control.

A thousand books, articles or speeches about self-defense by the oppressed could not have defined the situation as dramatically and clearly as the action in Oakland, California, one October morning in 1967. A shoot-out between two cops and two Black Panthers. One cop lay dead in the street. Huey P. Newton was under arrest, charged with his murder.

The Man tried to execute Huey. But millions of people —black people, white people, liberals, radicals, revolutionaries, housewives, doctors, students, professors—identified with Huey. They said black people *should arm themselves* against the violence of the pigs.

Huey's action redefined the situation for all of us and put the police on the defensive.

The Panther uniform—beret, black leather jacket, gun —helps create the Panther legend. Three Panthers on the street are an army of thousands.

The assholes of the California State Legislature met in Sacramento to pass a gun control bill directed at disarming the victims of the pigs—black people. So the Panthers drove to Sacramento to personally visit their congressmen. They brought their guns. They carried them into the statehouse.

The idea of armed mad niggers invading the Sacramento legislative chamber! The nightmare of every fat-cat congressman! Far-out guerrilla theater!

Fear and paranoia are the luxuries of suburban leftists, armchair intellectuals, graduate students, the uninvolved.

142

The further you are from the movement, the more scared you become. The Black Panthers aren't afraid. The yippies aren't afraid. The Viet Kong aren't afraid.

But in your living room, you're scared shitless. And that's just where the power structure wants you.

In the middle of a riot, I've never found anybody who's chickenshit. The way to eliminate fear is to do what you're most afraid of.

The goal of theater is to get as many people as possible to overcome fear by taking action.

We create reality wherever we go by living our fantasies.

25: George Wallace Is Bobby Kennedy in Drag

George Wallace is the highest flowering of Western culture.

He is the symbol of the country which destroyed the Indian, enslaved the black, colonized Latin America, A-bombed Japan, invaded Cuba and napalmed Vietnam.

He is the Amerikan flag. He is the cowboy, the Marine, the Bible-toting missionary priest, the businessman and the cop-on-the-beat.

Only one problem with ol' George:
He can't keep his fucking mouth shut.

George says out loud what the liberals are polite enough to say in the bathroom. Liberals get pissed at Wallace cause he's so upfront. He calls a spade a spade. Niggers are just plain niggers.

The only difference between liberals and Wallace is manners. George ain't got none.

So while liberals run the Vietnam war, exploit profits from Latin America and supervise the containment of black people, yippie George Wallace runs around stating the Amerikan ideology in theatrical terms. He blows the liberals' cover story.

We yippies must reprint Wallace speeches, get him TV time and open up offices for him all over the country. He's the best fucking Marxist rabble-rouser in Amerika today. He's *our* best organizer.

Wallace attacks niggers, students, hippies, demonstrators, pacifists, intellectuals, pot-smokers, commies, liberals. We make all kinds of distinctions between us. To Wallace there are no distinctions. He does his best to unite us.

The liberals try to get everyone freaked at Wallace so we won't notice that they do precisely what he advocates: Nazism comes to Amerika as liberalism.

Straight people get very uptight at Wallace: more freaked out by Wallace's *words* than by the liberals' *actions*.

We freeks know how to deal with Wallace: *we love him.*

The yippies went to Wallace's rally in the San Francisco Cow Palace wearing huge "STAND UP FOR AMERIKA" buttons and carrying picket signs demanding "More Bombs for Vietnam" and "Cut Their Hair."

We noticed fifty people in front walking around in a circle picketing the rally. I took a closer look and recognized the picketers—members of the Communist Party. "Bettina," I said, shocked, "how can you picket Wallace? He's done so much to build the Communist Party. Aren't you grateful?"

145

They continued to picket.

So we split and shouted over our shoulders at the commies: "WHY DON'T YOU TAKE A BATH AND GET OFF WELFARE?"

The yippies rose to their feet as Wallace appeared.
"*SIEG HEIL, SIEG HEIL, HEIL HITLER, HEIL HITLER!*"

"The next hippie who gets in front of my car will be the last hippie," said Wallace.

"*Kill 'em! Gas 'em!*" we shouted.
"*Send 'em back to Russia where they came from!*"
"*Send 'em back to Africa where they came from!*"

We were exhausted from waving the Amerikan flag and giving the Nazi salute all afternoon. We were the loudest motherfuckers in the whole place.

I looked around at the stadium packed with retired bankers and little old ladies. This is the right-wing menace? Fuck.

The right-wing menace exists—but it's not Wallace.

It's the Kennedy liberals.

*   *   *

The right wing is the left wing's best ally.

Who was the first person to call the battles at San Francisco State College "a guerrilla war—Vietnam at home?"

SDS?

Fuck no.

Ronnie Reagan!

(I can now reveal a secret. The last time I voted in an election, I cast my free Amerikan vote for the only movie star in the race, Ronnie Prettyboy.)

I dig fighting the right wing because they are upfront about what they do.

146

Wide World Photos, Inc.

They sensationalize, fantasize, and romanticize. To build *their myth* they exaggerate *our myth*—they create a Yippie Menace. The menace helps create the reality.

They turn *us* into heroes.

They set high standards for us to fulfill, and we become giants trying to fulfill their fantasies.

The right wing are our theatrical directors.

The right wing believes so intensely in their own bullshit that they are too stupid to deceive and govern effectively. Unlike the liberals, they don't know how to *divide-and-conquer.*

Martin Luther King's body wasn't cold thirty seconds before the liberals went on national TV saying what a great man he was. Why? Because he deplored violence *by black people.* So they tried to use King's image to *control* black people.

147

The yippies were so amazed by the liberals' change of heart toward King that we organized a "Martin Luther King Memorial Sit-in" in Mayor Lindsay's office to honor King's *methods*.

We invited a lot of white folks, including Lindsay, Humphrey, Nixon, Whitney Young and Roy Wilkins to attend the sit-in.

None of them showed up. Instead Lindsay sent 1,000 cops to surround City Hall to keep the yippies out.

Right-wing coverage of our demonstrations is hot, thrilling, mythic. Liberal coverage is cool and dull.

"Favorable" coverage by left-liberal journalists is patronizing and moderate without historical fancy or stereophonic scope. Outrageous attacks on us by right-wing fanatics has a touch of the spectacular and glorious.

Dig the *New York Daily News*, the largest underground paper in Amerika. They see the yippies as "SEX-DOPE-RIOTS." The humorless *New York Times* calls us the Youth International political party.

The right wing is usually right too. They use the right words: war, riots, revolution. The John Birch Society understands the world we live in better than fools like Arthur Schlesinger Jr. and Max Lerner who don't know what the fuck is happening.

We must *become* everything the *Daily News*, Birchers, Wallace, Buckley and your local right wingers say we *are!*

Amerika doesn't have the sniffles or a sore throat: she has malignant cancer.

George Wallace is Robert Kennedy and J. William Fulbright in drag as he proudly shows off the symptoms and the scars.

He helps us yippie surgeons develop the tools for the coming operation.

26: Are the Kennedys Assassination-Prone?

Gil and I were taking the tube back to the hostel one cool, pleasant, London night. We had just seen "Lawrence of Arabia." A man sitting nearby held a newspaper upside down with a gigantic picture of Jack Kennedy on the front page.

"What did Kennedy do?" We stood on our heads in the aisle to read the headline:

KENNEDY IS ASSASSINATED

"What kind of a joke is that?" Then we saw the name of the paper—the *London Communist Daily Worker*. These English commies have an outrageous sense of humor.

Back at the hostel, everyone was freaked out, huddling around radios, listening to the Voice of Amerika.

I thought to myself: "Kennedy—the jewel of Amerika: one bullet and the beauty, money, fame, power, a family dynasty are all gone." *Far out!*

The next day, the papers carried a full-page picture of the accused, Lee Harvey Oswald. I couldn't take my eyes off his bitter face. I had seen that scowl so many times in the streets of Amerika.

Lee's father split before he was born. He was raised by a mother who slaved day and night to keep him alive. Lee probably felt guilty for her slavery. He hated school. He joined the Marines, probably because the recruiting posters promised that he would become a man. He drifted from job to job and from city to city. He was like millions of faceless Amerikans, denied money, dreams and ambitions. We hear about them only when they kill rich men or rape rich men's daughters.

Many Lees live in Amerika. The tantalizing Kennedy myth is dangled before their noses every moment. "KENNEDY ANNOUNCES CANDIDACY." "KENNEDYS ATTEND FILM FETE." "JFK KISSES BLARNEY STONE."

Kennedy was told at birth that he was a "Kennedy." With that name, he was predestined for greatness.

Lee wanted to be great too, but everyone told him he wasn't for shit. At school they told him if he didn't get rich, famous and handsome he had only himself to blame.

Lee's biography had an important twist. He was a troublemaker in school and in the Marines. Pissed off, he went to Russia.

Who is Lee Oswald? With a rifle Lee forced the world to see. He found he could participate in the dream of Kennedy greatness only by killing a Kennedy.

A VISION

Lee climbs to the witness stand in the Political Trial of the Century to accuse Amerika of assassinating him at birth. He screams:

"Amerika, I'm tired of wishing I were a Kennedy! I'm tired of hating what I am! I am a man!"

Oswald then links his life to the sufferings of black people in Amerika and peasants throughout the world.

Who knows what divine madness boiled beneath that bitter scowl?

We will never know, thanks to the Dallas police, the Warren Commission and, of course, the CIA.

When he assassinated Robert Kennedy, Sirhan Sirhan consciously saw himself as an Arab patriot, representing oppressed peoples as he fired a pistol bullet, shattering the

myth of rich, white, Amerikan power. Amerika drives the exploited people of the world to become Lee Oswalds, Sirhan Sirhans, Viet Kong.

What dedication and fanaticism is inspired by Amerikan greed!

The Amerikan people dismiss Sirhan as a crazy, fucked-up, irrational extremist. But it is the extremism of Amerikan power and Kennedy power which drives her powerless people to such "extremism."

"What seems irrational from the viewpoint of the Mother Country," says Eldridge Cleaver, "may be rational from the viewpoint of the colony."

27: *Free the Prisoners and Jail the Judges*

Knock, knock, knock.

I'll never forget that knock. Soft and sexy. The timing was uncanny because I was just starting to roll a joint.

"Who's there?"

Silence.

"Who's there?"

Silence.

"Who's there?"

"POLICE. OPEN UP!"

I had a flash that an it-can't-happen-here experience was beginning to happen.

"Do you have a search warrant?" I said, feeling silly. The police were pounding on my weak wobbly wooden door, on the top floor of a broken-down tenement building off the Bowery, and I was asking about a search warrant.

Silence.

"What do you want?" I asked.

"OPEN UP. We want to talk to you about homicide in the Bronx."

Homicide is not my thing.

I opened the door a crack, and gangbusters, three huge motherfucking plainclothes pigs crashed in, flashing badges, blowing whistles, stumbling all over each other and throwing me up against the wall.

"All right—HANDS UP!" They reeked of beer.

"Where's your gun? Where's your gun?" they shouted.

"Do you have a search warrant?" I repeated, lamely.

"What do you know about a search warrant? What do you have in here that you shouldn't have?" They began to stalk me.

Jones, the potbellied one, twisted my arm and yelled,

"Where are the drugs? If you don't tell us where they are, and we find them, you'll be sorry."

Jones stood under the life-size poster of Fidel Castro on the wall. Images of niggers and commies raping his daughter zapped his brain and turned him into a crazy man.

"You commie!" he screamed. "You dirty commie! You dirty commie!" He ripped the Castro picture off the wall and lunged for me. **"I want just five minutes alone with you."**

"Nah, better leave him alone," said the other cop, Brown. They were into police vaudeville—hard cop/soft cop, just like in the movies. Brown was reading my address book and the letters on my desk. "Hey, this guy's really a subversive. Look at this shit."

Brown then flashed a piece of paper in front of my face: "Here's your search warrant."

They started ripping the place apart. It was like a World War II Nazi movie—only these guys weren't Nazis. They were typical white Amerikans. As Amerikan as apple pie. Amerikan soldiers raiding a Vietnamese village. White cops invading the black ghetto. Invaders from another culture.

"Bet you think we like Wallace. We don't. We like Goldwater. We didn't like Kennedy, but we didn't like what happened to him either."

"What are yippies going to do in Chicago, Rubin?"

"Hey, Rubin," said Jones, "I looked for you up at Columbia. You were up there, weren't you? We'll see you at the next demonstration. Yuk, yuk."

"Don't you have any patriotic magazines?" Brown asked. He moved like a tank through the papers in my desk.

"There's a copy of *Life* around here somewhere," I muttered.

"*Life!* That's a commie magazine."

I asked Brown to telephone Nancy and tell her that I wouldn't be meeting her.

He dialed the phone and said, "Nancy, this is a friend of Jerry's. He wants you to meet him at the ninth precinct. He's been arrested."

"Let's get out of here," Brown said. "I can't stand the smell any longer."

They assembled their little arsenal of drugs, handcuffed me and led me down four flights of stairs and into a small car, unmarked except for Amerikan flags pasted all over the windows.

"Don't worry," said Jones, "I won't hit you while you're handcuffed."

"You're lucky you're an Amerikan," said Brown, matter-of-factly. "If this was Cuba, you'd have no trial and they'd cut off your hands."

Jones looked at me with smoldering hatred: "*Someday we're gonna pick up all of you commies and put you in jail for good.*"

When Nancy arrived at the precinct, I shouted, "Nancy, it's a trap. Get out of here." But as she turned to run, two cops grabbed her.

The cops took both of us to 100 Centre Street for midnight arraignment. Jones kept muttering, "**I just want five minutes with you, you commie.**"

We entered the courthouse, and Jones took me down a long corridor alone. He kept pinching my neck and telling me to walk faster, slower, slower, faster, faster, slower.

At the end of the corridor I saw a black cop and felt less uptight. But Jones screamed to the cop: "This guy is a Communist. He hates Amerika. He loves Russia and China!"

Jones told me to walk into the cell. When my back was turned, he kicked me in the base of my spine. I fell to the floor in incredible pain. I could hardly walk. The other cops grinned.

It was a torture chamber. In another cell six cops were pounding the shit out of a guy in Army uniform.

I was charged with felonious possession of dangerous drugs; bail was set at $1,000. Charges against Nancy were dropped. My friends raised the bail in an hour, and I went from the jail to Bellevue emergency ward where X rays showed that I had a severely sprained coccyx.

Paul Krassner said that within five minutes after the bust thousands of toilets in a 25-block area flushed, causing a severe drought on the Lower East Side. No one could remember another bust of a pot-smoker in his home in the East Village: A truce exists between cops and pot-heads.

Pot laws are political. They're used to get the undesirables—blacks, hippies, Puerto Ricans, Mexicans, dealers, troublemakers, organizers, public nuisances. It was

155

obvious what this was all about: Chicago. We had been planning Chicago for months, and this was the counterattack.

But if the purpose of breaking into my place was to stop the yippie myth, it had the opposite effect. It was what we needed to unite and inspire us. The bust gave us a shot-in-the-arm. Somebody in the FBI is an undercover yippie.

The laboratory report identified the contraband as three ounces of grass and *non-narcotic* pills. I know the cops got at least five ounces of grass, some hash, three mescaline and four acid tabs. What nerve they have to tell me that my good drugs are non-narcotic!

"Hey, Bill," I said to my lawyer, Bill Kunstler, "if they aren't narcotic, why can't I have them back?" Bill laughed. The obvious explanation: The cops sold the rest. Narcotic cops are the biggest dealers in town.

I went to court 15 times over the next 10 months, each time to get a date for a new appearance. Going to court is like going to school. Keeps you off the street. Teaches you good manners.

At one of those routine appearances, the judge called my lawyer aside. "Marijuana?" said the judge. "What's so bad about marijuana? I smoke it myself.

"Tell this guy to plead guilty to a misdemeanor, and I'll sentence him to five minutes in jail, just enough time to be fingerprinted."

Minutes later I stood before the judge. He asked me, "Before you enter your plea, have you been told what sentence to expect?" That was my cue. The courtroom is theater.

"No," I mumbled.

"Speak up," he said.

Fuck, yes, I thought.

"No," I said.

Al Copeland

Then I pleaded guilty to misdemeanor possession of drugs and heard myself sentenced to five minutes in jail.

Justice in Amerika is a supermarket. Pigs arrest us for expensive crimes—and let us off pleading guilty to cheaper ones. Fucking deals. The judge is a poker player and the cards are other people's lives. It's blackmail. If we demand our constitutional rights—a jury trial—we pay even more heavily when found guilty.

159

The courtroom is a negotiating session between State and Criminal on how much the Criminal must pay for having been arrested. Ninety-five percent of the people busted make deals to get lesser punishments. The poor stand helpless in the face of the state's power. The rich get rich man's justice; the poor get poor man's justice. *As Lenny Bruce said, "In the halls of justice, the only justice is in the halls."*

I got sentenced to five minutes in jail because the D.A. knew there was no informer and their search warrant was a piece of shit. The Justice Department had admitted bugging my telephone—the FBI relayed signals to New York narcs. And the D.A. did not want to tangle with that master gladiator of the courtroom, Bill Kunstler, my attorney.

We troublemakers would be in deep shit if it weren't for our movement lawyers: fighters like Kunstler, Charles Garry, Len Weinglass, Arthur Kinoy, Beverly Axelrod, Irv Birnbaum, Jerry Lefcourt, Michael Kennedy, Faye Stender, Phil Hirschkop, Leonard Boudin.

Everyone else in the courtroom is playing a game. For the judge, it's a game. For the prosecution, it's a game. For nonmovement lawyers, it's a game.

But movement attorneys breathe, play, worry, fuck, suffer with us. When we are on trial, they are on trial. When we go to jail, they go to jail. They cannot afford to be cynical like everyone else in the courtroom. *They are defending their brothers.*

The movement must create two, three, many Bill Kunstlers and Charles Garrys so we can defend every person now shuttled cafeteria-style from the street to the courts to the jails.

Every arrest in Amerika is political.

We must take *every case* to the Supreme Court.

The first yippie act when we take power will be to open the jails.

Free the prisoners and jail the judges!

28: Sirhan Sirhan Is a Yippie

The Democratic Convention opens behind barbed wire. Props include tear gas and bayonet-bearing paratroopers, rushed back from Vietnam.

Millions mill in the street searching for the government they've lost. Their attention is drawn to the sky.

It's a bird.

It's a plane.

No, it's super-LBJ, airlifted into the besieged hall.

Suddenly a handkerchief is waved from an upstairs window.

The Democratic Party surrenders.

The yippies take over.

Ecstasy.

Vision ends.

The Festival of Life vs. the Convention of Death: a morality play, religious theater, involving elemental human emotions—future and past; youth and age; love and hate; good and evil; hope and despair. Yippies and Democrats.

The media prepared to transfix the consciousness of the entire world on Chicago for five whole days. *Our* chance to touch the world's soul. The right act at the right time: instantaneous communication. Nobody could pretend Chicago wasn't happening. Local disruption becomes global war between good and evil.

The mission: freak out the Democrats so much that they disrupt their own convention. And meanwhile demonstrate to the world the alternative: our own revolutionary youth culture.

161

The yippies got ready to drop our own hydrogen bomb on the Democrats—a free food and free rock festival.

Can you dig it! A free rock orgy bringing millions of young people from all over the country to Chicago? We expected every rock group in the U.S. and England to come: the Rolling Stones, the Beatles, Country Joe and the Fish, even the mysterious Dylan.

A free rock festival in Chicago meant liberating our own culture from the high-priced, walled-in dance halls, taking it away from the avaricious businessmen and making it free for the people in the streets and parks.

The impulsive beast of our bodies, the spirit of Pure Unprovoked Music, has been domesticated for profit. Fuck profit. Rock music must give birth to orgasm and revolution.

Yippie technologists were hard at work developing portable rock equipment so that we could fight cops and dance to rock music at the same time.

Yippies would paint their cars like cabs to pick up delegates at their hotels and drop them off in Wisconsin.

We would infiltrate the hotels as yippie bellboys to fuck the wives of delegates.

Yippies dressed like Viet Kong would hand out free rice and kiss babies in the streets.

And one night 100,000 people would burn draft cards at the same moment, the flames spelling out "BEAT ARMY."

Rennie Davis and Tom Hayden were ducking bombs together in a North Vietnamese bomb shelter when they heard Chicago would be the site of the Democratic Convention. Without a word they dedicated themselves to bringing hundreds of thousands of people to Chicago to stop the bombs at that moment dropping on their heads.

Dick Daley fell asleep every night drinking warm milk in bed, eating cream-filled cookies, scratching his crabs (which he got from his closed-door advisory meetings with J. Edgar Hoover) and reading bedtime stories entitled "The Best of Yippie."

New episodes were dropped off at his office every day at five o'clock by the Chicago Red Squad.

We gave the papers to an ambitious Red Squad recruit who passed them on to his boss, Sgt. Healy, who in turn gave them to Daley.

The yippies had 24-hour special delivery access to Daley's brain cells!

What emotions surged through Daley's tender head as he lay there in bed reading about fuck-ins, loot-ins, smoke-ins, LSD in the water supply?

He fucking freaked out.

He surrendered the entire battle to the yippies five months before the convention.

He went on national TV and said:

"I have conferred with the superintendent of police this morning. I said to him very emphatically and very definitely that an order be issued by him immediately and under his signature to shoot to kill any arsonist or anyone with a Molotov cocktail in his hand in Chicago because they're potential murderers, and to issue a police order to shoot to maim or cripple anyone looting any stores in our city."

Shoot to kill!
Maim!
Cripple!

Dick Daley tears wings off butterflies.
Dick Daley eats black man's flesh for breakfast.
*Dick Daley ******** little girls and ******** little boys.*

Yippie was flying high.

Kids asked each other, "Going to Chicago?" Plans spread by the greatest conspiracy of all—word-of-mouth.

Was Dylan coming? Sure!

The Beatles? Sure!

Rolling Stones? Yippie!

The Viet Kong sending a delegation? Sure!

The Pope coming? Why not!

Dr. Spock importing the suburbs? Outasight!

Martin Luther King marching? Sure!

Che? Right on!

Eldridge? Yippie!

Jesus Christ? Sure!

Absolutely!

We denied nothing. We embellished every rumor and passed it on to ten more people. Mail flooded into the yippie office from all over the country. What a monster we had unleashed! We were creating a bigger myth for Chicago than the Democrats were.

We knew our myth was catching on because everybody attacked us. SDS urged people to stay away in an article entitled, "Don't Take Your Guns to Town."

Every week we'd pick up the movement papers and see ourselves slaughtered in print: "Yippies—the Media Shuck."

Ralph Gleason, a paisley capitalist music critic, wrote: "If a kid is killed by a Chicago cop this August in this caper, then Jerry Rubin is as guilty of that kid's death as LBJ is of the dead GI in Vietnam."

One morning Nancy dreamed she got a phone call from Walter Cronkite.

"Daley is double-crossing us," Walter yelled.

"Cool down, Walter," Nancy said.

Cronkite began his weird tale: "Daley has just made a secret trip to see some of his buddies in the Kremlin. He's got this idea of having Russia invade Czechoslovakia on

165

the eve of the convention so that Daley will be free to kick the shit out of you guys. Then both Russia and Daley get away with it."

Nancy yelled over the telephone into Walter's ear:

Stephan Shames

Yippie!
Czechago was so big everybody wanted to get into the act.
McCarthy.
Kennedy.
HHH.
Even old LBJ himself.

LBJ called a press conference. He took out a white handkerchief and for a moment everybody thought he was going to make history by blowing his nose on nationwide TV. Instead he started waving his handkerchief and mumbling something about politics being "dirty."

LBJ WAS SURRENDERING TO THE YIPPIES! LBJ was dropping out of politics.

"Oh fuck," we moaned. "LBJ, baby, don't drop out." It sounded like LBJ was also going to announce that he was never going to get another haircut.

We started sobbing.

LBJ was a shrewd old yippie.

166

People stopped shouting, "Yippie!" The yippie office was deserted. Yippie buttons were discarded. No one cared enough to protect our files. Nobody cared enough to steal our files. The phone stopped ringing. The mailman stopped coming.

HHH added insult to injury, satirizing the yippies' "Politics of Ecstasy" by proclaiming the "Politics of Joy."

Kennedy was taking the "!" out of "yippie!" Like LBJ he conspired to destroy the youth revolution, but he was doing it by stealing *our* rhetoric and *our* symbols.

Even some yippies had hidden fantasies of Bobby Kennedy smoking pot in the White House.

"What if Bobby shows up at our Festival of Life and wants to dance?" some yippies wondered. With LBJ a hippie and Kennedy now a candidate, interest in Czechago went DOWN. Down. down. Bobby was bringing life back into the Democratic-Death Convention.

We considered dramatically throwing all our yippie buttons into the Atlantic Ocean in a public "Death of Yippie."

Nancy, Stew and I watched Kennedy defeat McCarthy in the California primary and then went to sleep. I was dreaming when the phone rang. "Jerry, Jerry, turn on the TV!" Tom Hayden's hysterical voice said at the other end.

"Kennedy's been shot."

I took one look at the killer's face on the screen. Shock of recognition swept my body.

Remember that quiet little guy who sat in the corner at that first yippie meeting to plan the Czechago festival?

The guy who didn't say a word the entire meeting. Who disappeared. Who was never seen again?

Sirhan, man, what the fuck have you done?

Sirhan Sirhan is a yippie.

29: The Battle of Czechago

Every Amerikan's first glimpse at the dawning of the 1968 Democratic National Convention:

Two hundred freeks running around the park. Funny-looking, longhaired, crazy yippie boys and girls, practicing Japanese snake-dancing and street-fighting with poles, learning how to defend themselves by kicking a cop in the balls with a well-placed karate blow while shouting:

"WASHOI!"

Czechago police are permanently stationed outside each water main in the city to prevent the yippies from dropping LSD in the water supply. The Democratic Convention is behind barbed wire.

And we are just warming up.

Sunday we looked around Lincoln Park and counted noses—maybe 2,000 to 3,000 freeks—and we organizers looked at each other sadly. We once dreamed 500,000 people would come to Czechago. We expected 50,000. But Daley huffed and puffed, and scared the people away.

Daley would not have succeeded without the movement's active cooperation. The entire movement in California scorned Czechago. SDS and the middle-class Peace Movement said, "Stay home." The only rock band to come was the MC5; the only folk singer was Phil Ochs.

Everybody feared a set-up: the Democrats deliberately chose Czechago in order to lure us there, kill us, put us into concentration camps and move into full-scale fascism.

So we looked around Lincoln Park at our brave few and sighed. "This is it."

But although we were few, we were hard core: after the movement/Daley fear campaign, who but a bad, fearless, strungout, crazy motherfucker would come to Czechago?

And we *were* motherfucking bad. We were dirty, smelly, grimy, foul, loud, dope-crazed, hell-bent and leather-jacketed. We were a public display of filth and shabbiness, living in-the-flesh rejects of middle-class standards.

We pissed and shit and fucked in public; we crossed streets on red rights; and we opened Coke bottles with our teeth. We were constantly stoned or tripping on every drug known to man.

We were the outlaw forces of Amerika displaying ourselves flagrantly on a world stage.

Dig it! *The future of humanity was in our hands!*
Yippie!

For six months we tried to see Daley about sleeping in his fucking parks. I also wanted to tell Dick that I thought he was a great actor and should get an Academy Award for his role as mayor.

But Daley kept sending his simple-minded flunkie, assistant mayor David Stahl.

And Stahl, true to his name, did nothing but stall.

Fruitless negotiations between the yippies and the city of Czechago finally ended with Allen Ginsberg singing *Hare Krishna* to Stahl.

So would they let us sleep in the park and cool the whole thing out? Or would they drive us into the streets, creating the very riot they said they sought to avoid?

A few days before the Death Convention, death descends suddenly.

On the streets of Old Town a yippie is shot through the heart by raving pigs.

A Sioux Indian.

Dean Johnson.

We stage a funeral march.

A black brother stands on the busy pedestrian street at the very spot where Dean died:

"Watch your step, sir, there's a dead man."

"Watch it, mister, you stepped on him." He points to the dried blood on the pavement, then to two bullet holes in the wall.

"Pardon me, sir, you just stepped on a dead brother."

Ever-present Czechago pigs crash in, nightsticks flailing.

Some were reluctant at first to call cops "pigs." "Pig" was a Berkeley-San Francisco thing, inspired by the Black Panthers. Also it was an insult to Pigasus. But we took one look at Czechago's big blue-and-white porkers: "Man, those fat fuckers really do look like pigs!"

"And two guns! They each got two guns! One for fast draw and one for slow draw!"

Czechago was the Wild West.

Sunday night a police car drove through Lincoln Park. From every direction the yippies' own brand of rock music started: the rhythm of rocks rending copcar metal and shattering windshields. The Battle of Czechago was on.

Creatures from the Smoky Lagoon, grotesque, massive machines like tanks lit with powerful lights, entered the park and shot tear gas that made you vomit.

Pigs with masks—looking like sinister spacemen—led the way, ghouls in hell, turning the park into a swimming pool of gas.

Yippies faced the Big Machine until the last minute. Then we split into the streets, shouting joyously: "The streets belong to the people!"

Yippies set fires in garbage cans, knocked them into the streets, set off fire alarms, disrupted traffic, broke windows with rocks, created chaos in a hundred different directions.

Police cars zoomed after us. We'd hit the ground, lying low, not making a sound until the cars passed by.

Police cars caught alone were wiped out with rocks.

You found a group of friends you could trust, and that became your revolutionary action cell. The streets provided the weapons. A tree's branch became a club. Rocks everywhere.

Citizens opened their doors to give us sanctuary from club-wielding porkers.

White working-class kids helped the yippies build barricades.

Black bus drivers on strike joined yippies in the streets throwing rocks at scabbing white bus drivers.

Reporters stood around taking notes and snapping pictures. They thought they were standing on the 38th parallel or something.

Whack! A pig cracked one right across the head.

Journalistic blood!

Crack! Another photographer goes down, blood staining his white shirt.

Crack!

"Hey, I work for the Associated Press."
"Oh, you do, motherfucker. Take that!"

By Tuesday yippies cheered reporters and photographers who showed up on the battle lines. Merely to appear in the riot area was an act of bravery. We shared bandaged heads.

The word flashed across the world: The Democrats are the party of blood, pigs and cruelty: PIGS vs PEOPLE. Every pig was a law unto himself in the streets.

Government authority had broken down so much that we had no recourse except to take our struggle to the United Nations. The yippies declared themselves a "new nation," demanding self-determination.

Stew showed his stitched head at an international press conference and demanded that the United Nations Security Council be convened and that a U.N. peace-keeping mission be sent to occupy Czechago immediately.

U Thant received our demand by telegram two hours later. We received a mimeographed response *three months later* that the request had been directed to one of the UN's 20,003 committees.

The pigs invaded the sanctity of Lincoln Park on Tuesday morning to arrest Tom Hayden and Wolf Lowenthal. We rushed to picket the jail and ended up in an assault on General Logan's statue in Grant Park. We hoisted the Viet Kong flag high upon the statue.

"It's better than Iwo Jima," someone shouted.

Hundreds of pigs rushed up to recapture the hill.

On Tuesday yippie guerrilla strategy scored its greatest victory. Tear gas aimed at yippies floated into the ventilation system of the Hilton Hotel.

The Hump was in bed when he smelled something funny.

It was tear gas! He had to stand under the shower 45 minutes to get all the stinky, stingy tear gas off.

The headlines blared:

HUMPHREY IS TEAR-GASSED.

Our guerrilla strategy was working: if they tear-gas us, they tear-gas themselves too.

Wednesday's rally of sleepy "the war is immoral, illegal" speeches was halted when the pigs saw the Amerikan flag being lowered. The lowering of the red-white-and-blue, while not illegal, is a symbolic attack on the masculinity of every Czechago pig, so they attacked us with gas and clubs and were met with an avalanche of rocks, bags of shit and table benches.

Then 10,000 people began an illegal march to the amphitheater and were stopped by a line of pigs.

We ran through the streets toward the Hilton Hotel, but every bridge to the Hilton was blocked by National Guardsmen who volleyed tear gas at us as we approached.

"HERE! HERE!" someone shouted. "An unguarded bridge." Through some colossal military fuckup by the pigs, we flooded across the undefended bridge to the front door of the Hilton. We filled Michigan Avenue.

The pigs got the order to clear us out and, as TV floodlights turned the dark street into the world's Broadway, cops shot tear gas, clubbed reporters, pushed little old ladies through store windows, smashed faces and tried to annihilate us.

Yippies built barricades, started fires, turned over paddy wagons and spread havoc through the streets. The Hump's nomination took place at the precise moment the Nazi state carried out its brutal attack on the people.

Scenes of pigs beating McCarthy housewives, newsmen and photographers, liberal college kids, yippies, delegates and innocent bystanders were perpetuated on videotape.

Scenes of brave youth battling back flashed over and over again on every TV channel: *infinite replay of the Fall of Amerika.*

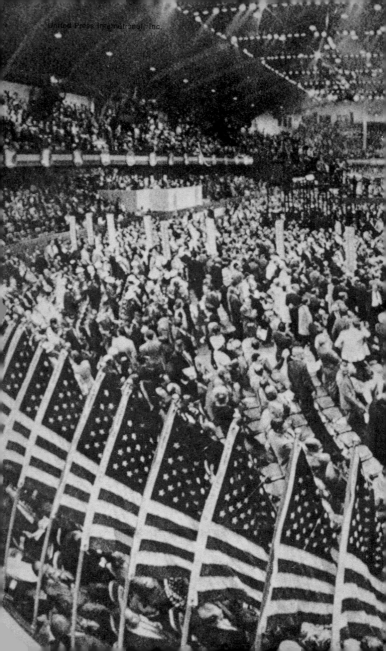

30: The Nomination and Election of Pigasus, the Pig, as President of the United States

Pig buttons, pig bumper stickers, pig ads in *The New York Times*, pig campaign offices all over the country!

Far out!

Everybody kept asking us, "We know what you're against, but what are you for?" Finally we found something to be for: a pig for president!

At last, a positive program!

Our campaign slogan: *"Why take half a hog when you can have the whole hog?"*

We could see the yippie festival now: a dramatic mock convention with potsmoke-filled caucus rooms and delegates from Middle Earth, Aquarius, New Mexico and the Lower East Side.

"The delegation from Telegraph Avenue gives fifty votes . . . to the pig!"

The masses cheer.

But the candidacy of the pig threw the yippies into heavy factional fighting. Some yippies wanted to kill Pigasus at a gigantic pig roast for everybody to eat. The Democrats nominate their presidential candidate and *he* eats *the people*. We nominate our candidate and *we* eat *him*. We devour our candidate before he devours us.

Only one political issue could divide the yippies. We had no problems with capitalism (against), Albania (for), free sex (for), ABM (for). But vegetarianism almost destroyed us.

Nobody objected on the basis of pigs not being kosher, even though yippies are Jewish hippies. But Ed Sanders refused to have any part of a political party that was going to take the life of any beating heart.

Open war broke out when we arrived in Czechago. I got pissed off when Abbie went off to a farm and brought back a cute, white, tiny little Petunia Pig. "Our Pigasus has got to be the smelliest, most repulsive hog that ever stunk up the earth! Just to look at him has got to make you puke," I said.

The yippies had a showdown that almost came to blows and public denunciations. Through the pig we were trying to define yippie. Was yippie trying to make Amerika laugh? Or was yippie ready to blow Amerika up? Abbie and Paul agreed to keep Petunia out of the presidential sweepstakes if we could find an uglier pig.

We didn't know anything about pigs. I heard that Jim of the Head Shop once lived on a farm. I called him up and asked him if he knew anything about pigs. "A little," he said, and the next day we piled into a car, $25 in our pockets, and we were on our way to heartland Amerika, rural Illinois, to buy the next president of the U.S.A.

The first hog farm we came to had 400-pound hogs.

Were they ever beautiful!

I mean ugly! They were so ugly they were beautiful. They were perfect presidential material.

One even had the face of a Supreme Court justice.

The more a pig weighed, the uglier he was. Also the hotter. If we took a 400-pound pig into the city, he'd have a heart attack and die. What about the theater of our candidate dying in the middle of his acceptance speech at the Picasso statue! Could Amerika psychologically handle the death of yet a fourth major public figure?

We arrived at a second farm and saw pigs in all ages and sizes. We started laughing. We laughed so hard our insides hurt. Did the Big Wheels of the Democratic Party have as much fun picking their candidate? We wished we could bring the whole sty to Czechago. *I mean pigs really do need a bath.* They offend the sensibilities.

We met the man in a straw hat who ran the farm. "I hear a lot of demonstrators are coming to Czechago this week," he said. That's how he saw the Democratic Convention. When I heard that I knew we'd won before the battle had even begun.

We told him we needed a pig for a school play. We pulled out $25. "Take any one you want," he said. Fifty black-and-gray pigs were running around. Man, they were dirty. And, fuck, they smelled like pigshit. The farmer told us to catch our own. We looked at each other, uptight; none of us ever had the opportunity to chase a pig before.

The pigs were uptight too. They ran whenever we approached. So we chased pigs until we backed one into a corner. Jim held him by the tail while we all got ahold of him. He was six months old and weighed 200 pounds. The new presidential candidate was ready to begin his long descent to the White House.

We all crowded together into the truck. It was hot. Pigasus jumped up and down ferociously. Every 10 minutes we had to pull into a gas station to pour water over him. He kept screeching and freaking out. But he didn't mess with us once. I learned a heavy lesson: *Four-legged pigs aren't violent.*

The goal was to take Pigasus to the Picasso statue in Civic Center a few days later to declare his candidacy. Lawyers told us we would violate a disorderly conduct statute by bringing a farm animal into the city. What if Humphrey were bringing Ringling Bros. Barnum & Bailey Circus into the city as a publicity stunt? Would they arrest Hubert? All laws are political.

Could we get Pigasus to Civic Center before the cops snatched him? We had set up a big international press conference, so the cops were hip to it. It would be a coup for the cops to pick up Pigasus first; thwarting the dramatic myth that would go across the world.

178

The police, expecting some of us to go pick up the pig, parked outside the house where we slept. So we got up early one morning and took the cops on a wild pig chase, while another car quietly went off to get the pig.

The scene at Civic Center was packed with TV, radio, newspapermen and FBI agents. The car with the pig arrived, and yippies began singing, "God Bless Amerika," while herding the screaming pig into the Civic Center Plaza.

Ten two-legged Czechago pigs grabbed us before Pigasus could utter *one oink*. "Democracy is bullshit in Amerika!" I shouted as we were grabbed. "They won't even let our candidate make his own acceptance speech!"

They threw seven of us into a paddy wagon and slammed the door. Then they opened the door again and threw in Pigasus. We rode to jail with our candidate. We were waiting to be fingerprinted when a fat Czechago cop entered the room and said, "Gentlemen, I have bad news. All of you face pretty heavy charges.

"The pig squealed on you."

Pigasus dominated everyone's consciousness during the Democratic Convention. "Well, he's as good as all the other candidates," said a waitress, a typical response to Pigasus' campaign promise of garbage. But the Pig angrily accused the United States government of rigging the election against him. His basic campaign demand was that everyone in the world should be allowed to vote in the Amerikan election because Amerika controls the world.

We demanded Pigasus be flown to the Texas White

179

House immediately for foreign policy briefings like all other candidates. We demanded Secret Service protection.

Instead, wherever Pigasus tried to campaign—in San Francisco, New York, even London—he was busted. Each time we just went to a farm and got another candidate. Pigs are just like Democrats and Republicans: one is as good as another.

Some people say the yippies are a put-on. Who was a greater put-on, Pigasus or McCarthy? McCarthy told us to cut our hair and go back into the system to get votes for him to end the war.

That didn't work, so McCarthy got down on all fours and told his supporters to vote for the Hump.

Pigasus, true to his word, supported no other pig but himself.

After living through a lot of experiences with Pigasus, including arrest and incarceration, the yippies grew fond of Pigasus.

We insult four-legged pigs when we call policemen "pigs." Four-legged pigs are not violent or sadistic. They just love to roll around in their own shit and eat it.

They're hedonists—with bad taste.

What are pigs but yippies on a lower scale of evolution?

Brown Bros.

31: My "Bodyguard" Turns Out to Be a Czechago Pig

Spain

Sunny was eight inches taller than I. She had tattoos on her arms and legs.

I didn't need a bodyguard. But the idea of a giant blond chick bodyguard vibrated good theater.

Sunny looked down at me and said, "Don't worry, Jerry. I got a piece."

She pointed to her purse.

Two minutes later Sunny introduced me to Bob. He was dressed in a black leather jacket, black T-shirt, black vest, boots, black helmet, sunglasses and a two-day beard.

Bob and Sunny hung around for a while. They brought me ice cream.

Bob kept telling me to eat and sleep well.

He told me to take care of my health.

He was like a Jewish mother.

"By that time, it had been several days since I'd had a bath and the stench alone was enough to put me in solid with the demonstrators."

He was a drag.

One night we were together when the cops shot tear gas into Lincoln Park, and Bob zoomed off like a scared motherfucker.

I gave him a powerful pill and told him to go home. It was a drug 1000 times more powerful than acid. Bob swallowed the pill, jumped on his motorcycle and roared off into Yippie-Trip Land.

"I arranged with my police contact to leave notes in the men's room in Lincoln Park, because many of the yippies don't bother to use toilets, but dispose of their human waste out in the open."

Ten P.M. Wednesday. The last remaining warriors were running through the streets escaping from the cops after the Battle of the Hilton. We ducked into a restaurant. A suspicious man walked behind us.

We started running down the street.

Suddenly a car careened up, and four men jumped out.

"Jerry Rubin, Jerry Rubin, we love you," one guy yelled.

"I'm going home," I muttered.

"We'll take you home," they shouted, grabbing me by the hair.

Nancy was thrown aside. "You want to come too, sister?"

They forced me into an unmarked car and sped away.

"We're going to put you in a bag and drop you in the river, Rubin."

"Whenever you're on the streets, Rubin, there's trouble."

One porker radioed: "We got Jerry Rubin."

They took me to pig headquarters. A small room, the public office of Amerika's political police, the Red Squad—those overweight dudes who hang around the fringes of demonstrations

182

with cameras and tiny tape recorders, sport shirts falling over their pants to conceal their guns. They try to act real chummy to us ("Hi, Tom! How you doing, Martin!") while they collect dossiers and plot our destruction.

They shouted questions at me:

"Who won, Jerry? Who won?"

"You guys ever take baths?"

"You each have your own girl friends or do you sleep with each other's?"

"What are you going to do if you take over the government?"

"Why not get your guns and fight it out now? We're ready."

"You communicate with the Chinese commies?"

"Jerry, do you like Czechago? You're gonna be in jail here for a long time," said the Top Red Squad Pig.

"How could I have caused the riots—I know personally only a couple of hundred people in Czechago?" I said.

"How many people do you know?" Pig said.

"A hundred and twenty-four."

"It shoulda been a hundred and twenty-three," he replied.

Cops packed into the small room to get a front row seat for the midnight theater. There were about 30 in the room.

Suddenly appearing at the door, looking at me with cold, hard, freaked-out eyes was Bob, slick-haired, clean-shaven, dressed in a suit.

A few hours later I was charged with a felony, "solicitation to commit mob action," on Bob Pierson's testimony—and jailed on $25,000 bail, more than the bail for accused murderers.

The *Chicago Tribune*'s banner headline the next day blazed:

HOW COP SPIED ON THE YIPPIES: UN-SHAVEN, UNBATHED, HE INFILTRATED TOP RANKS TO GAIN SECRETS, MADE BODYGUARD AND CHIEFTAIN.

The *New York Daily News* revealed that Bob copped my "secret diary" and "turned it over to his superiors after Pierson picked a 'fight' with another officer, was knocked down and placed under arrest."

Then came the December issue of *Official Detective Stories:*

"*EXCLUSIVE!* BEHIND THE YIPPIES' PLANS TO WRECK THE DEMOCRATS' CONVENTION."

with Bob's own sensational fantasy about how he became my "bodyguard":

"A fight broke out near where we were loafing and I waded in and broke it up, sending the combatants scattering in different directions.

"I knew that Jerry Rubin was nearby and that was my main reason for intervening. I demonstrated to him that I was not afraid and that I was tough.

"Within an hour there was another fight—also within Rubin's sight—and I broke that up, too.

"The third time that afternoon, the combatants were a little tougher and not so easily frightened. However, because of my size and my previous training, both as a policeman and as a counterintelligence agent, I knew tricks of fighting that these tough young men didn't.

"Before I could stop this fracas, I had to

"The girls wore dresses with nothing under them and to give photographers a thrill, they raised their dresses above their heads. The boys unzipped their pants and exposed themselves to passersby."

184

administer beatings to three different men. By the time I was through with them, they had a healthy respect for my ability.

"All this was witnessed by Jerry Rubin—I had entered the fray for his benefit, though he didn't know it—and he was so impressed that he conferred with [Abbie] Hoffman, who agreed to let me go so that I could become Rubin's personal bodyguard."

"The last couple of days I was home before going underground I carefully avoided bathing."

Bob eliminated Sunny from his superacid hallucination, because there's nothing very mythic about taking advantage of a chick. Sensational battles and beatings make better prove-your-manhood myth. Sunny had to skip town because Pierson busted her on a felony.

"I joined in with the chants and taunts against the police and provoked the police into hitting me with their clubs. They didn't know who I was, but they did know that I had called them names and struck them with one or more weapons."

"If these were children, where were their parents? Why weren't they at home, instead of in a far-off city with the avowed purpose of stirring up trouble?"

An undercover cop is some trip! To glorify his own fantasy, he glorifies the people he spies on and makes us 1,000 feet tall.

Pierson turned us all into Superfreeks, capable of taking more dope, fucking more chicks, killing more pigs, blowing up more buildings and throwing more shit than all of the regular freeks in the world put together.

If there is ever a Hollywood movie about the yippies, Bob Pierson should write the screenplay.

Big Bob is a yippie.

He takes his fantasies for reality.

32: *How Amerikan Airlines, Richard Nixon, Spiro Agnew, Strom Thurmond, John Mitchell, Walter Cronkite, CBS, NBC, ABC, Uncle Ho and a Million Spirits Conspired to Burn Czechago Down*

Dig Pavlov and his dog Spot:
Ring the bell and then give Spot food.
Soon Spot salivates when you ring the bell.
Conditioning.

Aided by thousands of mercenary psychologists from the universities, Madison Avenue got the Amerikan people in the 1950's to salivate whenever they heard the bell: "Communism."

"The Negro people have been given a raw deal for centuries, but the Communists are using the Civil Rights Movement, so we got to stop them."

The politician rings the bell. The people froth and quiver. So much for Negroes. Next problem?

"South Vietnam is no democracy like the United States, but the Viet Kong are Communists, so the Vietnamese are better dead than red."

The politician hits the bell, and the Amerikan people slobber all over their red-white-and-blue bow ties.

But then a Wonderful Thing happened. *Children were born*. Children were born who get no bad vibes when we hear the name "Stalin."

We get sexually aroused by the word "revolution."

We get high on "yippie."

And we puke at the sound of "Nixon."

The government is frantic to find the *word* to make the Amerikan people drool again. They even have a semanticist named Hayakawa carrying out big-scale fieldwork at San Francisco State College.

They're trying out a lot of words.

The most popular one now is *"conspiracy."*

They arrested seven Berkeley radicals for *conspiracy* to commit a misdemeanor—trespassing—during Stop the Draft Week. Conspiracy to commit a misdemeanor is a felony: dig the semantics!

They busted teenagers in Toledo for *conspiracy* to smoke dope.

They busted the cast of Lennox Raphael's "Che" in New York for *conspiracy* to commit consensual sodomy.

Twenty-one New York Black Panthers were arrested for *conspiring* to blow up department stores and the Botanical Gardens.

And they arrested Black Panther Bobby Seale, Dave Dellinger, Tom Hayden, Rennie Davis, Abbie Hoffman, Lee Weiner, John Froines and me for *conspiring* to cross state lines to eat suckling pig in Czechago.

According to yippie semanticists, "conspiracy" comes from the Latin root meaning "to breathe together." Our crime is that we breathe. The crime becomes a felony when we breathe together. The seriousness of the felony mounts as more people start breathing together at the same time in the same place.

We *are* The Conspiracy. We're the biggest, baddest motherfucking Conspiracy you ever saw.

We got everybody on our side. Dig all the people who worked with us conspiring to plan the Czechago police riot.

The first conspirators were the airlines. Amerikan, United and TWA flew all of us there *youth fare.* All you need to fly youth fare is long hair. All longhairs look alike. Posing as my 20-year-old piano student brother Gil, I traveled from New York to Czechago a thousand times to further the conspiracy.

Richard Nixon, Spiro Agnew, Strom Thurmond and John Mitchell got so excited that they gave us $500 to send our first yippie statement across the world.

But for real money, we went to the TV networks. We offered each network exclusive information about where scenes of police violence were going to occur. ABC refused to bid, but CBS and NBC fought like dogs.

We gave Brinkley and Cronkite auditions repeating the line: Czechago is a police state." Cronkite made it sound more convincing, so we accepted his bread.

The network executives agreed their reporters would be physically beaten by Czechago cops in order to personalize the media's involvement with the story.

And there was Ho, who conspired with Dave Dellinger via International Telephone and Telegraph (every inch tapped and retapped by the FBI), to arrange the Viet Kong seizure of the Amerikan Embassy in Saigon to inspire our Czechago recruits with a will-to-win.

We sent the Justice Department a long list of conspirators to help them with their indictments for Czechago.

Top of the list was Dylan—we learned it all from him.

> *The pump don't work*
> *cause the vandals*
> *took the handle*

What about Gene McCarthy? The yippies had a secret meeting with Gene one week after he entered the New Hampshire primary. We told him he was going to raise naive hopes and cause a riot of outraged young straight people in Czechago. He dug it. (We sent a tape of that discussion to the Justice Department.)

Fuck, Danny the Red set France on fire three months before Czechago to shoot us up with adrenalin. And Mythic Mark Rudd Conquered Columbia to set the revolutionary dynamics in motion.

If the FBI wants to bust those who really created Czechago, they have to indict Caryl Chessman, Charles Van Doren, Marilyn Monroe, Oswald Augustus Owsley, Sherman Adams, Walter Jenkins, Bobby Baker, Tim Leary, Gary Powers, Antonin Artaud, Abe Fortas, Sputnik, Allen Ginsberg, Jimmy Piersall, John Dillinger, Norman Mailer, the Marquis de Sade, Charlie Chaplin, Mary Jo Kopechne and Lassie.

Any list of conspiracy indictments must include everybody possessed by the spirit of freedom. But out of trillions, they selected only us eight.

And they forgot to indict those who conspired to create our conspiracy: Dickie Nixon and Dickie J. Daley.

The Conspiracy is a spirit dwelling in the land. It is bigger than all of us together.

People in Berkeley were walking down Telegraph Avenue one fine day, and without warning they were touched by the Revolution. The Conspiracy spirit moved to the Pentagon where people .became transformed by the spirit of Berkeley. And then to New York. Czechago. France. Back to Berkeley. Everywhere!

Magic!

The Conspiracy is Cosmic.

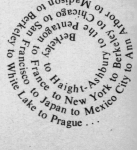

Berkeley to the Pentagon to San Francisco to France to New York to Berkeley to Chicago to Madison to Ann Arbor to Mexico City to White Lake to Prague . . . to Japan to Haight-Ashbury

190

33 : The Academy Award of Protest Acceptance Speech

This is the greatest honor of my life. It is with sincere humility that I accept this federal indictment. It is the fulfillment of childhood dreams, climaxing years of hard work and fun.

I wish to thank all those who made it possible: my mother, my father, my woman Nancy, my brother Gil and Louise, Stew and Gumbo, Abbie and Anita, Sharon and Robin, Spartacus, Tom Paine, Pun and Genie, Ho, Max Scherr, Jeff and Alice, Lenox, Fidel, Jim Retherford, Marshall Bloom, Tuli, Keith and Judy, Wolf, Bob Scheer, Phil Ochs, Huey, Eldridge, Lenny Bruce, Pigasus, Paul Krassner, Ed Sanders, Che, Martin Kenner, Abe Peck, Walter Cronkite, and last but not least—Richard J. Daley.

I realize the competition was fierce, and I congratulate the thousands who came to Czechago. I hope that I am worthy of this great indictment, *the Academy Award of Protest.*

With my indictment I join the list of outstanding world figures who have crossed state lines to create civil disturbance: the Beatles, Elvis Presley, the late Marilyn Monroe, Jim Morrison, the President of the United States and Joe Namath.

And you know who else is guilty? The hippies who dressed in psychedelic Indian clothes, boarded British ships and threw tea overboard in 1773! They crossed state lines with intent to destroy property.

Congress passed the antiriot law as a warning to the game of football. Fans who cross state lines, and then tear down the goalposts, are subject to arrest.

The crime is not in the act, but your INTENT at the moment of crossing state lines. It's against the law to think bad thoughts while crossing a state line.

You can even break this law in your own home! A telephone call to someone in another state is enough. Or a letter. Or an interview on radio/TV which is broadcast from one state to another.

The yippies broke the antiriot law when we mailed a postcard to Daley telling him that we were going to put LSD in the water supply!

You don't even have to be at the scene of the riot itself. You can jet-plane into a town, give a speech and then jet 10,000 miles away. If a riot takes place after your speech, no matter where you are, you're guilty of "causing" it.

You can break this law without violence or damage to property.

A riot is defined as a "*threat of* violence or a *danger of* damage to property."

The yippies in Lincoln Park were a riot. So is a baseball crowd. A Beatles concert is a hell of a riot.

Where does one draw the line between "free speech" and "inciting to riot"? It's fairly simple.

If your speech is *ineffective*, it is protected by the Constitution.

If your speech is *effective*, you are "inciting to riot."

Effective speech—speech which moves people—is against the law.

Since crime prevention is an essential aspect of law enforcement, the antiriot law requires a husky Police State for its enforcement.

a: Jim Retherford (Ernest Weekley); b: Ed Sanders (Frank Pearson); c: Stalin (Wide World Photos); d: Gumbo Clevir (Al Copeland); e: Julius the Just (Wide World Photos, Inc.); f: Marilyn Monroe (Wide World Photos, Inc.); g: Mao (Wide World Photos, Inc.); h: Paul Krassner (Roz Payne) (Wide World Photos, Inc.); i: Dylan (Wide World Photos, Inc.); j: Mario Savio (Wide World Photos, Inc.); k: Phil Ochs (Wide World Photos, Inc.); l: Lenny Bruce (Wide World Photos, Inc.); m: Huey P. Newton (Wide World Photos, Inc.). n: Louise Kurshan and Gil Bailes or Mom and Dad or Susan and

The FBI is forced to tap our phones, sort through our garbage and read our mail in search of violations before they happen.

How far off is the day when the FBI sets up checkpoints at state borders, examines "passports" and prohibits entrance to potential "rioters"?

Congress was in a mood described best as "mob rule" when it passed this law in 1968. The fires of Detroit and Newark were still smoking. Racist Southern congressmen wrote and lobbied for the antiblack bill, screaming that riots were fomented by a national conspiracy, agitators traveling from state to state, International Communism.

The purpose was to jail Stokely Carmichael and Rap Brown. Congress hallucinated that there would be no riots if there were no agitators!

Amerika thinks the "solution" to racial oppression is to pass laws against those who fight the oppressor.

As the Walker Report documented, the cops rioted. Our long hair incited cops to riot. We are indicted under the federal antiriot law because our long hair incited cops to violence against us. These indictments are the personal responsibility of Richard Nixon. They were delayed for weeks waiting specific and individual approval from the White House.

They represent a vicious attempt by the government to try to use punishment to stop demonstrations. But the major result of these indictments will be to excite every young kid across the country to want to cross state lines and become a "rioter" by the time he's a teenager. Yippie!

34: Yippie-Panther Pipe Dream No. 2

The Yippie-Panther pact began spiritually in 1964 and 1965 when Berkeley students were disrupting their university and stopping troop trains—and Eldridge Cleaver was in Folsom prison.

Eldridge writes in *Soul on Ice* how he felt: "I'd like to leap the whole last mile and grow a beard and don whatever threads the local nationalism might require and comrade with Che Guevara, and share his fate, blazing a new pathfinder's trail through the stymied upbeat brain of the New Left . . . I'd just love to be in Berkeley right now, to roll in that mud, frolic in that sty of funky revolution."

Eldridge Cleaver had been sentenced to jail at birth by White Amerika. His first prison sentence was for possession of what he calls a "bag full of love" (marijuana), but his crime was his black skin.

Now he sat in jail and read about the children of his white jailers spitting in the face of their arrogant fathers!

The oppressors' children joining the oppressed!

Don Lewis

Five years later, Eldridge Cleaver became candidate of the Peace and Freedom Party for President of the United States.

Eldridge's vision was coming true: young whites rejecting white society. "White" was a state of mind. Hippies were seeking a new identity.

Young whites were blowing middle-class Amerika out of their minds and bodies with drugs, sex, music, freedom, living on the streets. They were filling the jails. They were

195

not in the revolution merely to "support" blacks, but were dropouts of white society fighting for their own freedom.

Eldridge wanted an alliance between bad blacks and bad whites. Criminals of all colors unite.

Brotherhood through common struggle and oppression. Equality-under-the-pigs.

Black-white unity becomes a real thing *only* when whites are treated like blacks.

Al Copeland

Eldridge wanted a coalition between the Panthers and the psychedelic street activists. He had one requirement for his vice-presidential candidate: he had to be out on bail.

I had just been attacked in my apartment by three New York narcs. So Eldridge called me, and I dug it.

But what would the Peace and Freedom Party say? They'd have a heart attack.

It's made up of whites who do not feel oppressed, who are waiting for the working class to rise up, whose props are suits-and-ties, leaflets and position papers.

These whites can accept running a pot-smoking, gun-toting, ex-con nigger for president.

But a longhair white freek for vice-president?

Heaven forbid!

I went to the New York convention of the Peace and Freedom Party and threw my hat in the ring.

I suggested that we move the Peace and Freedom Party out of their bureaucratic offices and into the streets. A party of white dropouts.

I got creamed.

The party nominated a college professor with an attaché case.

Eldridge could not find one person in the California Peace and Freedom Party to support an alliance with the yippies. People would just laugh. "Eldridge, you're not serious."

But Eldridge would not let the Peace and Freedom Party bureaucrazy put a lock on his mind—any more than the pigs.

At the founding conference of the Peace and Freedom convention in Ann Arbor, Eldridge broke the boredom by

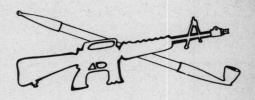

putting on a yippie button and nominating a yippie for vice-president.

Stew described the reaction in the *Barb*:

"I saw women crying and grown men driven to distraction. The mood on the convention floor was crazed and could best be summarized by the look on the face of one up-and-coming young college professor who, when he careened head-on into Eldridge's chest eye-level with a yippie button, stuttered and said, 'My God, it's true! How could you?' "

Eldridge later told the *Barb* what happened: "You would've thought I'd thrown a bomb. Their class prejudices came out when they talked about having to explain people like the Up Against the Wall/Motherfuckers, yippies and hippies to the rest of the white community. They talked about them as 'those scum.'

"The cultural revolution in the white community is to the left of the political left in the white community."

The Peace and Freedom Party voted to nominate no national vice-presidential candidate, rather than accept a yippie who was at that moment preparing to destroy the Democratic Convention in Czechago.

Eldridge and the yippies got together next, high in the Berkeley hills, to smoke a lot of grass and write the Panther-Yippie Pipe Dream:

Opening Salvos from a Black/White Gun by madmen grappling with the cause of their madness in search of a cure. We have been driven out of the political arena into the wilderness of our own dumb minds. We will not dissent from the Amerikan government. We will overthrow it.

—Eldridge Cleaver, Stew Albert, and Jerry Rubin, *Joint Introduction*.

The symbol of the Yippie-Panther pact is a hash pipe crossed by a gun.

Eldridge, Minister of Information of the Black Panther Party, wrote:

"Into the streets! Into the alleys! Back of town! Onto the rooftops! Behind whatever shelter remains for a black person here in Babylon! . . . Brother Malcolm said that it's gonna be the ballot or the bullet. Let us join together with all those souls in Babylon who are straining for the birth of a new day. A revolutionary generation is on the scene.

"There are men and women, human beings, in Babylon today. Disenchanted, alienated white youth, the hippies, the yippies and all the unnamed dropouts from the white man's burden, are our allies in this cause."

Stew and I, for the Youth International Party, wrote:

"Vote with your feet on election day. Can you dig it: in every city boycotts, strikes, sit-ins, pickets, pray-ins, feel-ins, piss-ins at the polling places . . . Nobody goes to work. Nobody goes to school. Nobody votes. Everybody becomes a life actor of the street.

"Force the National Guard to protect every polling place in the country. Join the rifle club of your choice. Freak out the pigs with exhibitions of snake dancing and karate at the nearest pig pen. Release a Black Panther in the Justice Department.

"Fly an Amerikan flag out of every house so voters can't find the polling places.

"Take a burning draft card to Spiro Agnew."

Eldridge was the craziest presidential candidate Amerika's ever seen.

On the steps of Sproul Hall, he led 5,000 Berkeley students in a chorus:

"FUCK YOU RONALD REAGAN!"

"FUCK YOU RONALD REAGAN!"

At the Panther-Yippie Erection Day rally Eldridge smoked a joint, poured out his soul to 3,000 people and then withdrew his name from the presidential campaign in favor of Pigasus.

As the heat of the parole board got heavier and heavier on his head, he got more and more courageous. He was like a man who had risen from the depths of hell and despair to know what a joy it was to be alive—and free.

He tempted the pigs until the day before Prison Day and then split, telling us:

"See you soon, by fair means or foul."

"No nigger on parole ever got away with the shit that I got away with. I ran for President. I wrote a book. I insulted every politician in Amerika. I've traveled around the country and called them all pigs. And I'm going to do it again. I'm going to come back. I'm happy. I had a lot of fun. I loved it. And we got to raise the shit to a higher level."

Amerika has to jail Eldridge Cleaver because freedom is contagious—and Eldridge is a *free man.*

Amerika declared war on humanity when she exiled Eldridge.

If Amerika is not free for Eldridge Cleaver, Amerika has no right to exist.

The pigs fired the first shot.

But we, the white and black niggers, will fire the last.

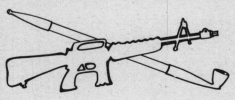

35: HUAC Digs Che's Painted Tits but Bars Santa Claus

One morning, early September, 1968, Abbie called me from New York.

"Just got a HUAC subpoena," said Abbie. I immediately felt that old sexual anxiety again. Subpoenas envy.

"You did? **I want one, too**!"

I phoned HUAC's West Coast confidante, a Hearst newsman named Ed Montgomery.

"Jerry, baby," he said. "Just talked to HUAC. They've got a subpoena for you. They've been looking for you in New York."

"New York?" I said, deliriously happy. "You guys are sure doing a shitty job of trying to save this country! I've been in Berkeley all week!"

I wanted to turn the receiving of the subpoena into a religious ceremony. HUAC must have liked the idea too, because they agreed to deliver the subpoena in Sproul Plaza at noon, the busiest time on campus.

"The dream of every red-blooded Amerikan boy and girl should be to grow up and become a subversive and get subpoenaed before HUAC," I told a crowd of students, reporters, TV cameramen, cops and FBI agents, as Tom Hayden and I sacrificed our subpoenas to the God of Fire. I wore 10 Eldridge Cleaver for President buttons.

"Last time I was subpoenaed before HUAC I made four hundred bucks and lived on it for two months, organizing demonstrations on the Berkeley campus. I want to thank HUAC. We're going to use the money we make this time to continue to finance the revolution."

The right-wing *Berkeley Gazette* said, "Rubin, in a mood of jubilation, seemed more to be accepting an invitation to a tea party than a summons to testify."

After the burning I hung around day and night on Telegraph Avenue pushing a "What-should-Jerry-Wear?" contest.

The Revolutionary War costume was really an attempt at rational communication with HUAC. I wanted this uniform to go beyond the heads of HUAC and straight to the kids. Maybe when they call me to testify, I'll rip off all my clothes and shout, "I have nothing to hide."

Maybe I should come as a baseball player with YIPPIES written on the back of my uniform? I'll bring a bat and ball and say to HUAC, "Let's go outside and settle this the good old Amerikan way!"

Eldridge suggested that I come dressed as a Black Panther and he come with me dressed as a hippie, but the parole board wouldn't let him travel.

Maybe come as a pirate?

A clown?

An Indian?

Then a fantastic idea hit me: Why not a little bit of everything?

Why not a gestalt?

I'll come as a one-man international revolution, a walking conspiracy.

My nonverbal message: Amerikan youth must begin guerrilla war. We must all become stoned guerrillas.

When guerrilla war comes to a country, it comes through the *style* of that culture. When guerrilla war comes to Amerika, it will come in psychedelic colors. We are hippie guerrillas.

YIPPIES!

I arrived wearing a Black Panther beret with Panther and yippie buttons, Egyptian earrings, a Mexican bandolier with live 303 British Infield bullets around my chest, black silk Viet Kong pajamas, jangling ankle bracelets, beads and a headband. I had cowbells and jingle bells around my neck, wrists and ankles so that every time I moved I sounded like an orchestra. My face, naked hairy chest and bare feet were painted with psychedelic designs and peace symbols. Over my shoulder I carried a toy M-16 custom-made rifle, the kind the Viet Kong use after stealing them from the Amerikans.

"Let me see that gun."

The guard at the door was a big fucking pig.

Rat-tat-tat-tat-tat! I shot him with my toy gun (just to show him it wasn't real).

Then he said, "Let me see those bullets. Hey, these are real bullets!"

"But," I said, "I got no gun to shoot them in."

"Well, you can't enter with these bullets."

Within seconds two pigs grabbed me by both arms and were dragging me down three flights of stairs and out of the House Office Building.

They wouldn't let me back in until I disarmed myself of the bullets. But they allowed me to keep my rifle.

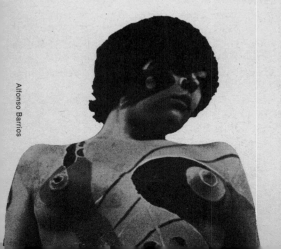

Alfonso Barrios

203

Guess what pissed HUAC off the most?

The Viet Kong black pajamas?

No.

The gun?

No.

The jangly bells?

No.

My painted tits!

Congressman Richie Ichord, the new chairman of HUAC, couldn't take his eyes off my painted tits. He really had a thing for my painted tits. He was more uptight about my painted tits than he was about political ideology.

Here we were, terrorists, anarchists and freeks. We had just executed the crime of the century in Czechago. And these HUAC assholes were talking about meetings of the Communist Party decades ago. They kept mentioning names of people who were dead.

I yelled out, "The Communist Party opposed the Czechago demonstration, fools!"

The gavel came pounding down. They didn't want their theater confused with facts.

Abbie raised his hand. *"May I be allowed to go to the bathroom?"*

We could feel the earth vibrate with the giggling of the kids who read that in their hometown newspapers. *The Profound Question of the Times.*

One morning I put on my blue-red-yellow Viet Kong flag as a cape. Abbie wore a shirt made out of the Amerikan flag. We split for the hearings at the House Office Building.

Cops massed about a block ahead of us. We saw them gripping their clubs and eyeing us the way cops do when they're about to move. They came toward us.

Then it flashed: I am about to be arrested for treason, for wearing the flag of the enemy in Washington, D.C.!

But who did the cops grab and toss into the paddy wagon?

Abbie with his Amerikan flag!

I was left standing all alone on the street with my VC flag.

"You Communists!" I screamed. "Traitors! This is the Viet Kong flag! What's happening to this country!"

The big day: My undercover cop was the scheduled witness. He was still hallucinating from that superpill we gave him. He said so many groovy things!

He said the yippies had an outasight trade agreement with a Czechago biker gang, the Headhunters. The yippies gave the Headhunters dope and sex. In return, we got dynamite and bike power.

He said that I quoted Lenin whenever I wanted to convince anyone of anything, that I suggested that we isolate the cops and kill them and that I advocated the assassination of Daley and McCarthy.

"Pierson did not say whether Rubin intended this as a direct threat for immediate action or whether it was a personal boast," reported the *Washington Evening Star*.

That night I returned to my hotel to find my room full of tear gas. A calling card and death threat from the Amerikan Nazi Party was tacked on my door.

My own HUAC testimony was all prepared. When they asked me to name members of the yippies, I was going to read them all the names in the Czechago and Washington telephone books.

I planned to hand each HUAC congressman $10 and cordially thank him for his hard work on behalf of the yippies.

I was going to give Ichord the same pill we gave Pierson.

And I planned to conclude: "There is an international commie conspiracy and it's four-fifths of the world and it's all against you, you dumb motherfuckers. You *should* be paranoid.

"I just took LSD, mescaline, STP, THC and marijuana and I'm flying high. I'm fucking stoned. And if you've never been stoned, you'll never understand what I'm telling you.

"You old motherfuckers are pissed off because we're stealing your children. There's even a Communist conspiracy in your own sperm."

Just as I was getting ready to testify, Ichord canceled the hearings for two months.

* * *

In two months I had my same old political problem: What to wear to Congress?

It was Christmas!

SANTA CLAUS!

Santa is a Red. He represents the Red Peril.

And he's got a beard, therefore he's a hippie. I'd be a red-bearded Santa Claus because I got a red beard.

And what does Santa smoke in that pipe? Grass!

Santa gives everything away free. He's a commie. Santa is a stoned commie.

Santa laughs a lot. At the hearing I'd get up and laugh, "Ho, Ho, Ho Chi Minh, the Viet Kong are gonna win; Ho, Ho, Ho Chi Minh, Ho, Ho, Ho."

I arrived at the hearing room in a rented Santa suit, and the pigs stopped me: "You can't come into the hearings unless you take off that silly suit."

I replied, "This is how I dress every day. You shouldn't be prejudiced against me because of the way I dress."

HUAC let me in with painted tits and gun, but they wouldn't let me in as Santa Claus.

I sat right down outside the hearing room. A couple of HUAC secretaries brought me cupcakes and told me that they dug the yippies. They didn't like working for HUAC.

We have infiltrators everywhere.

The next day's headlines blared:

HUAC BARS SANTA CLAUS.

I got high seeing that. I had communicated with every four-, five-, six- and seven-year-old kid in the country. I proved to them that the U.S. Congress was against Santa Claus.

Ichord told the *New York Daily News* that if he called me for future hearings "he would first recommend a competent psychiatric examination."

A month later HUAC proposed a new law outlawing insults to Congress through "cultural means."

What are cultural means? Dig it! Freaky clothes!

That's my law! I wrote that law.

I'm a legislator.

Once upon a time only congressmen could get laws through Congress. Now the average citizen can write laws.

That should be everybody's goal. Write your own law. Do something so crazy that they got to pass new laws to outlaw it.

They don't have enough laws now to stop what's going down.

Make them *outlaw you.*

Make yourself illegal!

36: *Burn Down the Schools*

David Fenton/LNS

A sunny day on the Berkeley campus. Students are carrying ten pounds of books from one class to the next.

We nonstudent fuck-ups say, "Excuse me, student. Did you know the sun is shining?"

They look at us like we're crazy.

We invade libraries yelling, "The sun is shining! The sun is shining!"

We go into a psychology class on "Thinking," a huge lecture hall with 300 students. The professor is up front, diagraming behavior on the blackboard. Everybody writes down in their notebook every word he spews.

His first words are, "Good morning, class."

The guy next to me copies down, "Good morning, class."

Somebody raises his hand and asks: "Do we have to know that for the exam?"

The classroom is an authoritarian environment. Teacher up front and rows of students one after another. Do not lose your temper, fuck, kiss, hug, get emotional or take off your clothes.

The class struggle begins in class.

We roll a few joints and start smoking in the middle of the classroom. The smell is overpowering, but no one seems to notice it.

The Viet Kong could attack with mortar shells, and everybody would still be taking notes.

It's an assembly line.

The professor talks; students copy.

Everyone is 99 percent asleep.

Marvin Garson takes off his shirt and begins tongue-kissing with his chick Charlie. I rip off my shirt and start soul-kissing with Nancy.

There we are in the middle of the class, shirts off, kissing, feeling each other up and smoking pot.

Everyone gets itchy and nervous because of us. No one can take notes any more. The professor stutters. Pens stop. People squirm. Everyone's looking at us—no one at the professor. But the students are too repressed and shy to say anything.

Finally a girl in the middle of the room can't stand it any more. "Could these people please stop making a disturbance?" she pants.

Nancy leaps to her feet: "This is a class on thinking! We're thinking! You can't separate thinking from kissing, feeling, touching.

"We're the laboratory part of the class. Anybody who wants to come, join us. Anybody who wants to listen to the lecture part of the class move to the other part of the room."

The professor then reveals his soul. "In *my* class," he says with authority, "*I* do the teaching."

Scratch a professor and find a pig.

(His assistant goes to get the uniformed pig, so we split.)

TWO HUNDRED PSYCHOLOGICAL TERRORISTS COULD DESTROY ANY MAJOR UNIVERSITY— WITHOUT FIRING A SHOT.

Schools—high schools and colleges—are the biggest obstacle to education in Amerika today.

Schools are a continuation of toilet training.

Taking an exam is like taking a shit. You hold it in for weeks, memorizing, just waiting for the right time. Then the time comes, and you sit on the toilet.

Stephan Shames

Ah!
Um!
It feels so good.

You shit it right back on schedule—for the grade. When exams are over, you got a load off your mind. You got rid of all of the shit you clogged your poor brain with. You can finally relax.

The paper you write your exam on is toilet paper.

Babies are zen masters, curious about everything.
Adults are serious and bored.
What happened?
Brain surgery by the schools.

I lost my interest in books in literature class. I lost my interest in foreign languages in language class. I lost my interest in biology in biology class.

Dig the environment of a university! The buildings look like factories, airports, army barracks, IBM cards in the air, hospitals, jails. They are designed to wipe out all individuality, dull one's senses, make you feel small.

Krystyna Neuman

212

Everyone should bring dayglow paint to campus and psychedelicize the buildings as the first act of liberation.

"Critical" or "abstract thinking" is a trap in school.
Criticize, criticize, criticize.

Look at both sides of the argument, take no action, take no stands, commit yourself to nothing, because you're always looking for more arguments, more information, always examining, criticizing.

Abstract thinking turns the mind into a prison. Abstract thinking is the way professors avoid facing their own social impotence.

Our generation is in rebellion against abstract intellectualism and critical thinking.

We admire the Viet Kong guerrilla, the Black Panther, the stoned hippie, not the abstract intellectual vegetable.

Professors are put-ons, writing and talking in fancy, scientific, big motherfucking words, so the people on the street won't dig that they're not saying shit.

They're so thankful for their "intellectual freedom in Amerika" that they're not going to waste it fighting on issues like poverty, war, drugs and revolution. They insist upon the freedom to be irrelevant.

We judge our teachers as men first and teachers second. How can you teach us about World War I if you weren't in the streets of Czechago?

The goal of the revolution is to eliminate all intellectuals, create a society in which there is no distinction between intellectual and physical work: a society without intellectuals. Our task is to destroy the university and make the entire nation a school with on-the-job living.

School addicts people to the heroin of middle-class life: busy work for grades (money) stored in your records (banks) for the future (death). We become replaceable parts for corporate Amerika!

School offers us cheap victories—grades, degrees—in exchange for our souls. We're actually supposed to be happy when we get a better grade than somebody else! We're taught to compete and to get our happiness from the *un*happiness of others.

For us education is the creation of a free society. Anyone who wants to teach should be allowed to "teach." Anybody who wants to learn should be allowed to "learn." There is no difference between teachers and students, because we teach and learn from each other.

The professors and the students are the dropouts—people who have dropped out of Life. The dropouts from school are people who have dropped into Living. Our generation is making history in the streets, so why waste our lives in plastic classrooms?

High school students are the largest oppressed minority in Amerika.

We know what *freedom is* when we hear the bell dismissing school.

"School's out, I'm free at last!"

Teachers know that unless they control our toilet training, we'd never stay in class. You gotta raise your hand to get permission to go take a shit. The bathrooms are the only liberated areas in school.

DROP OUT!

Why stay in school? To get a degree? *Print your own!* Can you smoke a diploma?

We are going to invade the schools and free our brothers who are prisoners. We will burn the buildings and the books. We will throw pies in the faces of our professors.

We will give brooms and pails to the administrators so they can be useful and sweep the place up. Fuck bureaucrats, especially the "nice" Deans of Men who put one hand around our shoulders while the other hand gropes for our pants. We'll take all the records, grades, administrative shit and flush it down the toilet.

The same people who control the universities own the major capitalist corporations, carry out the wars, fuck over black people, run the police forces and eat money and flesh for breakfast. They are absentee dictators who make rules but don't live under them.

Universities are feudal autocracies.

Professors are house niggers and students are field niggers.

Demonstrations on campuses aren't "demonstrations" —they're jail breaks. Slave revolts.

The war on the campuses is similar to the war in Vietnam: a guerrilla people's war.

By closing down 100 universities in one day, we, the peasants, can level the most powerful blow possible against the pigs who run Amerikan society.

We'll force the President of the United States to come on his hands and knees to the conference table.

We're using the campus as a launching pad to foment revolution everywhere.

Ronnie Reagan, baby, you're right!

37: "Welcome Home, Jerry!"

"Dear Jerry:
I fully agree with Mr. Brokamp in his decision inasmuch as I personally have for some time felt very deeply that your program of destruction for the sake of destruction is sheer nihilism whose open and avowed advocacy before a high school student body, as you requested, would be a rank contradiction of terms regardless of *where* or *when* it occurred."

The writer of this shit was my high school teacher and adviser to the *Chatterbox* when I was sports editor and coeditor.

I wanted to come back to speak at my old high school.

Fuck, I considered myself one of the high school's finest graduates. I was the only member of my graduation class specifically *not* invited to the 10th-year reunion of my class. The motto of the school was: "Rise to the Highest!" and I got myself a federal indictment. How much higher can you go?

But the new warden of the school, Ray Brokamp, said I couldn't speak because "it would defeat the school tax levy coming up for election next month."

I called Brokamp from New York and told him he better bring the National Guard to stop me.

Twelve years since I had been back in Cincinnati: Had the youth revolution reached the bowels of Amerika?

The banning of my speech was a good sign; the principal was uptight about something. Maybe he feared the students would really burn the school down?

The school looked exactly as it had when I left it. High on a hill, with a green dome. The place where the rich groom their kids into the social elite.

A giant banner hung from a second-floor classroom: "WELCOME HOME, JERRY!"

Students poured out of the building. They asked me for my autograph.

Plainclothes cops surrounded the school; FBI agents were on the roof with walkie talkies. It was the Pentagon all over again!

The warden of the prison came out flashing his best toothpaste-commercial smile and asked me to be "reasonable" and not to create an "incident."

"The decision that you cannot speak on school grounds is out of my hands," he said. "It has been taken up by the Board of Education."

The school had sure changed! It had all the signs of the revolution sweeping Amerika—from an underground paper to a full-time cop patrolling the halls. A thirteen-year-old led the fight against the principal's ban on my speech.

The president of the Student Council was a longhair, Andy Schwartz, who refused to carry the Amerikan flag during school assemblies. He wore a sign on his shirt saying: "Rubin—Forbidden Fruit."

217

And even the principal had a picture of a pot-head hanging on his wall—GEORGE WASHINGTON.

I left the campus very slowly walking three steps at a time, forcing the principal to keep shoving me gently from behind. "Please leave, Jerry."

A small army of FBI and plainclothes cops were poised to attack and arrest me for corrupting the morals of youth.

I slowly walked off campus leading 1000 students, TV cameras, reporters, cops and CIA agents to a nearby home where everybody got high, rapped and conspired to save our bodies from the fucked-up school system.

I arrived in Cincinnati on the same day a Teens for Decency rally was taking place. We held an Indecency rally on the grass in Eden Park.

The Decency rally opened with 10,000 people reciting the Pledge of Allegiance and singing "The Star Spangled Banner." Marching bands offered music. Off-duty cops provided the color guard. Bare-chinned politicians, judges and businessmen crowded the stage, arms held high, reciting prayers to God and Country. Kids arrived in buses paid for by their parents.

Across town 3,000 freeks contorted their bodies to the

orgiastic passion of live rock music while passing joints and sandwiches. The only adults around were the pigs. There were no buses paid for by parents—instead kids said: "I'm gonna get killed when I get home."

"You bear such a burden because of the actions of the indecent few," TV doll baby Dick Clark told the Decency rally, unaware that at that precise moment some indecent yippies in short hair were passing through the Decency crowd collecting spare change in red-white-and-blue containers.

A deathly pall fell over the Decency rally when a 19-year-old rally organizer, Bill Blue, took the mike and confessed his mortal sin: he forged a professor's name on a college form.

Shame!

But Bill asked for forgiveness—and the crowd waved their Amerikan flags to symbolize the acceptance of his apology.

Ecstatic cheers and foot-stomping shook the Indecency rally as we made Bill Blue honorary chairman of the Indecency rally for his great accomplishment—forging a professor's signature! We even forgave him for apologizing.

219

The Indecency rally was the weirdest mix you could find anywhere in Amerika. Kids from the richest suburbs in town. Kids from the poorest white and black ghettos. Kids from homes of workers. Businessmen's kids. Kids from Protestant, Catholic and Jewish homes.

The Decency rally ended with group chants:

"DOWN WITH OBSCENITY!"

"UP WITH GOD!"

"STAMP OUT FUCK!"

(Even the Decent want a chance to say fuck.)

That night a TV announcer said, "There were more people at the Decency rally, but they seemed to be enjoying themselves more at the Indecency rally."

The station bleeped out my voice every time I uttered what the announcer called "an obscene four-letter word," creating a nice audience-participation game.

"Motherfucker has 12 letters. Prick has five. Ah, shit has four letters. So has fuck.
"It could be shit or fuck, Helen."

My homeward odyssey next brought me to a house full of relatives, aunts and uncles, their kids and friends.

Uncle Sid greeted me at the door. He had his hair combed in bangs, wore a headband, a Mexican hippie vest and cowboy boots, and carried a small Amerikan flag in one hand and guitar in the other.

"You came too soon!" he said. "I was going to be sitting in a lotus position meditating."

Then he looked at me very disappointed. "Jerry," he said. "Where's your Viet Kong flag? The family deserves the whole costume."

"Uncle Sid," I laughed, "you were the first yippie."

I never realized to what extent we freeks dominate the consciousness of middle-class Amerika. They turn on the TV news and all they see are riots, student demonstrations and revolution.

Sid's son, Billie, is a longhair who just ended a hunger strike at Ohio State over ROTC on campus.

My landlord relatives have all been hit with paralyzing rent strikes.

"What's it all coming to, Jerry, what's it all coming to?" they moaned over and over again.

I dug it.

I visited the newspaper where I worked for five years as sportswriter and youth page editor. Scripps-Howard's brightest young journalist transformed into a dope-smoking, shaggy-haired, unbathed, riot-inciting, commie freek.

The reporters were sitting at their desks just like I left them 13 years ago. They arrived at work at the same time. They got a Coke from the same Coke machine at the same time. They took a shit at the same time. They took the same bus to the same house.

I used to say to them: "This paper oughta be a family. We should share all the bread and make all the decisions together."

"Jerry," they trembled. "That's Communism."

So I became a commie while working for the Cincinnati Post and Times-Star.

But 13 years later, there was a big difference: all the young reporters were getting no satisfaction. They wanted to drop out.

They crowded around me, hoping that I—an outlaw —had some solutions. They were at the bottom of the paper and had no desire to go to the top.

Soon I expect them to disrupt the very paper they work for with strikes, sit-ins, sabotage.

The editor refused to see me.

"I have no business with Jerry

he said.

But most of my old friends, the reporters, were warm and friendly. Great people. It wasn't their fault everything was so fucked up. It was the institution's fault. We have to overthrow the institutions and liberate the people.

I came back to Cincinnnati to freak out the city.

I told the press that the Youth International Party, the SDS and the Black Panthers were moving their national offices to Cincy, that Eldridge Cleaver was hiding out there, that I was moving back to the city to run for mayor and to "subvert the high schools with dope, sex and dynamite."

The papers were full of far-out letters asking why I wasn't arrested for, as one letter put it, "spewing forth a steady stream of lugubrious, seditious and salacious junk at young people."

The city manager gave the city's official reply:

"An administrative judgment was made that to arrest Mr. Rubin for a misdemeanor with a slight penalty would probably give him the confrontation he sought to appeal to the sympathy of the youth."

to transact
"Rubin"

Right on!

I drove through my old neighborhood. Once white, middle class and Jewish. Now a black community. The whites have fled deeper and deeper into fancy suburbs.

But look! The children of the fleeing middle class are hippies and are moving back into the old beautiful homes their parents deserted.

We are standing Amerika's myths on their heads. Remember Horatio Alger? We play his movie backwards:

WE BEGIN AT THE TOP
AND WORK OUR WAY DOWN
TO THE BOTTOM.

Cincinnati!

I was so glad to be home.

So many freeks on the street!

Blacks and longhairs giving each other the clenched fist.

Schools and institutions falling apart.

The poor cop-on-the-beat, businessman, churchgoer—they have lost their kids and their country.

Only a revolutionary can feel at home in Amerika today.

38 : *People's Park Will Rise Again*

The Central Intelligence Agency began to study maps, police reports, wiretapped discussions and newspaper files on the "Berkeley problem" in 1966. It was considered as important to roll back the liberated area of freeks in Berkeley as it was to secure South Vietnam from the Viet Kong.

Roll back Berkeley!

In an airport hideaway in San Francisco on September 11, 1966, a secret meeting was held to plan a new long-range operation to "pacify" Berkeley. Present were representatives of the CIA, the FBI, University of California officials, the state's top businessmen, officials from the Defense Department, five California police chiefs and Berkeley businessmen.

The plan? Simple! Take away the sea from the fish.

The "outlaw element" thrived in all the low-cost housing that surrounded the university, the old, rambling Berkeley homes.

The University of California, which played the major role in the CIA's insidious conspiracy, planned to buy all the low-cost housing, rip it down and build in its place dormitory buildings and IBM cardboard apartment houses— too high-priced and esthetically revolting for the nonstudents.

We'd have no place to live and would have to leave Berkeley.

The university began by buying the square block of land right behind Telegraph Avenue and three blocks from campus. They tore down all the old buildings to build dorms: completely unnecessary because 30 percent of the current dorms were uninhabited.

The nonstudents were pissed off when the bulldozers arrived. We knew what the goal was: "Hippie removal." We went on our way, muttering.

Al Copeland

Then the wonderful contradictions of capitalism fucked up the CIA's scheme. War came to the university with strikes, tear-gassing and armed occupation of the campus by the National Guard.

The state legislature freaked out. Uptight at university officials for not killing the rioters, they slashed state aid to the university. Gone was the money needed to build the dorms.

The land languished as a big mud puddle—a parking lot in the day, a mosquito breeding swamp at night.

Then one day a freek looked at the dismal bog: A VISION FLASHED INTO HIS HEAD!

He ran to see his friends. They mimeographed leaflets.

Within an hour 300 people were at the swamp. Bulldozers arrived to flatten the land. Rocks were shoveled up, green sod laid. After one day's work, a small section of the swamp had been transformed into a park.

A park!

A PARK BY THE PEOPLE!

The word went around Berkeley: come and see the new park. A notice was printed in the *Barb*. Money was collected on the streets. The next day 600 people were shoveling up rocks and laying sod.

While Ronnie Reagan was reading movie magazines at home, and while the entire university administration was drunk, sucking each other off in the back rooms of the university, people came to create People's Park.

Like a Chinese commune, thousands scraped cement from old bricks which others then used to create winding mosaic paths.

One group built a barbecue.

Another created a playground.

Some people made music on cans and drums, guitars, flutes, harps, recorders, voices and bodies.

Others made films.

Free food every day. Rock bands played.

It was a theater for the free play of creativity, energy and community. All of the art and life force of the underground culture swelling in pure love.

Within five minutes after you'd go to the park, you'd be stoned.

free food.
free work.
free sex.
free smiles.
free sun.
free moon.
free love.
free theater.
free store.
free music.
free dope.
free living.
free park.

Every day middle-class people from the Berkeley hills left their children to play with us. People came to the park to plant their own trees.

Hippies, students, yippies, fraternity boys, sorority girls, Panthers, middle-class people, everybody grooved in their own park.

"Hey, can I plant a corn patch?"
"It's up to you. You decide."

"Hey, can I put some swings in?"
"Outasight."
There was no Master Plan. Nobody gave orders. Some people wanted to turn the huge pit in the middle of the park into a swimming pool; others wanted to have a fish pond. Everybody working on the park got together in a town meeting and debated it for a few hours, and voted to have the fish pond.

The university deans woke up and saw what was happening. People were creating a park near the university! Motherfuck! That would attract all kinds of filth and vermin.

Ronnie was telephoned, and he zipped up his pants and rushed to a secret meeting. Two CIA agents were flown in from Washington.

What to do to stop these longhaired beasts from creating a base in the heart of the area the university was trying to destroy? The students had expropriated land valued at 1,300,000 dollars!

One morning at three A.M. Berkeley police arrived and shoved 50 people out of the park, making way for workmen who began to build a fence. By dawn a barbed-wire fence, lined with pigs, surrounded People's Park.

A noon rally at the campus resulted in thousands of people roaring down Telegraph Avenue to *tear that fucking fence down.*

Al Copeland

Hydrants were opened up.

Rocks thrown at pigs.
Pigs released tear gas.
People climbed on roof tops to throw rocks, and police pulled out shotguns!

The critical escalation in the war between the cultures: For the first time police opened fire on white Amerikan dissidents, shooting with birdshot. At the end of the day, James Rector was dying in a hospital, another man was blinded and at least a hundred people were wounded.

The National Guard turned Berkeley into an occupied city.

Curfew.

Vietnam helicopters stalked the city on reconnaissance missions looking for Viet Kong (anyone on the streets) to direct pig cars to club, attack and arrest.

Helicopters bombed the campus with tear gas.

Public gatherings were outlawed. People were tortured in jail.

People's Park became the base camp for the Occupational Forces in the war against the natives.

Tents replaced our playground.

Tanks and troop carriers ripped the trees and shrubs and flower beds.

Crude Army boots destroyed the green grass.

Beer cans and cigarette butts floated on the pond.

And Old Glory proudly flew above the carnage.

229

39: It's Against the Law
to Pee in the Streets

The revolution satisfies deep human needs denied by Amerikan society. That's why it's so dangerous. The biggest social problem in the country today is loneliness.

"What are you doing tonight?"
"I don't know, Marty, what are you doing tonight?"

Loneliness is not an individual problem—it's the collective problem of millions of Amerikans, growing out of the alienating environment we live in. We work in one part of town with people who are not our friends, and we sleep in another part of town and don't know our neighbors. We waste much of our life dying in mobile concentration camps called freeways or commuter trains.

Where in the city can we go to make friends? Where can we leap out of our individual prisons and enjoy each other? The city is full of walls, locked doors, signs saying

DON'T

If someone you don't know says hello, you get uptight: *"What's he want?"* It's taboo to talk to strangers. Everybody's hustling. The streets are paved with terror, the city a prison for the soul.

The car, a box, transports lonely people from the box where they sleep to the box where they work, and then back to the box where they sleep. Amerikans relate to each other as drivers of other cars; the only good driver is the one who takes another road. People killed on freeways are casualties of a war every bit as fucked up as Vietnam.

231

The streets are for Business, not People. You can't sit in a restaurant without buying food; you can't read magazines in a store—you gotta buy, buy, buy—move on, move on. What if you're in the middle of the city and suddenly you have to take a shit?

Tough shit.

We are liberating the city, turning the streets into our living rooms. We live, work, eat, play and sleep together with our friends on the streets. Power is our ability to stand on a street corner and do nothing. We are creating youth ghettos in every city, luring into the streets everyone who is bored at home, school or work. And everyone is looking for "something to do."

For us empty pockets means liberation—from draft cards, checkbooks, credit cards, registration papers—we are close to our naked bodies.

The hippie area becomes the first mass alternative to the Amerikan urban prison. Liberated neighborhoods are a great threat to capitalist city life. So the forces of Death— the business community, cops and politicians—conspire to wipe us out. An entire battery of laws—genocidal laws against the young—makes social life in the streets a crime.

If you don't hand a cop documentary proof of who you are, you can be arrested. To the state empty pockets means vagrancy.

Watching the world from a street corner is loitering.

Stephan Shames

Hitchhiking is a crime. It's against the law to panhandle, to rap to a crowd in the streets, to give out free food in the streets, to stop traffic. Playing a harmonica in the streets is illegal in Venice, California.

Two friends of mine were just arrested for the high political crime of pissing in the street. One was put into a mental hospital.

"Underage" kids caught on the streets are hauled straight to Juvenile Court.

And when all else fails, they establish a curfew, a Nazi law designed to prevent us from getting together.

These laws are designed to strike fear in the youth community. Although they exist on the books everywhere, they are enforced only in the ghetto. Cops patrol the hippie areas the way they patrol black communities, the way Amerikan soldiers patrol Vietnamese villages. Everyone is a likely enemy.

But the main strategy for destroying the free spirit is Business. "Psychedelic" stores try to steal the culture by selling fake artifacts to an emotion-starved Outside World. Camera-toting Amerikan tourists come through in buses and on foot, snapping pictures, laughing, squealing, pointing at us.

The streets turn into a hustle, a business section. We never know whom to trust. Burn artists and undercover cops flood the place, making it unsafe to buy or sell dope on the street.

We become an island in a capitalist sea attacked and infiltrated from inside and outside. The Death culture tries to destroy our Life Force and restructure the youth ghetto in its own image. We lack space in our own community— to breathe, conspire, celebrate, grow.

It is a war for land. Our survival depends on our ability to drive out the psychedelic exploiters, the invading pigs and the politicians and create youth communities where dropouts from middle-class Amerika can live.

Our goal is to create fires, blackouts, subway stoppages, strikes and snowstorms because only in crisis does liberation come to a city. People meet their neighbors for the first time while watching their apartment houses burn down. When the subway rumbles along, everyone acts as if no one else is aboard. As soon as there's a breakdown, people start talking to strangers. During snowstorms New York is a playground, an amusement park.

Crisis brings liberation to a city.

The revolution declares all land titles null and void. We are urban and rural liberators, seizing land for the people. No more "I own it!" People who believe they can own natural resources, industries or land are *really* candidates for mental institutions.

We will bring the war to the suburbs. The middle class creates suburbs as a sanctuary from the fire of the city. Children raised in the suburbs are treated as mentally and physically retarded. If we are not safe in our communities, why should corporate executives be safe in theirs?

We'll get our own tourist buses, steal cameras and ride through the suburbs squealing, laughing, snapping and pointing fingers.

We will take the revolution to Scarsdale.

In a revolution there are no sanctuaries.

234

40: We Cannot Be Co-opted
Because We Want Everything

Revolution is profitable.

So the capitalists try to sell it.

The money pimps take the best things our hearts and minds produce, turn them into consumer products with a price tag and then sell them back to us as merchandise.

They take our symbols, drenched with blood from the streets, and make them chic.

They own *our* music—the music produced by *our* suffering, *our* pain, the collective unconscious of *our* community! They put *our* music on records and in dance halls priced so high that we can't even afford to hear it.

Paisley rock promoters create fenced-in rock festivals, and pigs use tear gas and Mace to keep us out.

Beware the psychedelic businessman who talks love on his way to Chase Manhattan. He grows his hair long and puts on a brightly-colored shirt because "that's where it's at"—the money, that is. He has a big pile of cash and a short soul.

A hip capitalist is a pig capitalist.

The hip capitalists have some allies within the revolutionary community: longhairs who work as intermediaries between the kids on the street and the millionaire businessmen.

Beware the longhair who says he's more "revolutionary than thou" because he's "beyond politics." Beware the guru who thinks that his thing—be it scientology, astrology, meditation, vegetarianism, rock music or pacifism—will make the revolution *all by itself*.

Beware the longhair who lets himself get ripped off day after day rather than get bad vibrations.

Beware the longhair who defends the longhair businessman: "Shit, man, Bill Graham is just doing his own thing: making lots of bread."

They are traitors to their long hair.

All these tensions within the youth culture are reaching the boiling point because we are creating liberated areas for dropouts in every city and town, and because a community that doesn't control its own economic base is helpless in the face of The Man!

Haight-Ashbury, the first mass experiment at an urban youth ghetto, floundered because it had a Communist ethic built upon a capitalist material base.

Love cannot exist without economic equality.

In our community each man is his own brother's keeper.

Our youth ghettos must have a communal economy so we can live with one another, trading and bartering what we need. A free community without money.

We will organize our own record companies, publishing houses and tourist companies so profit will come back into the community for free food, free rent, free medical care, free space, free dope, free living, community bail funds.

Thousands of us have moved from the cities into the country to create communes. Dig it! The communes will bring food into the city in exchange for services which the urban communes will bring to the country.

We will declare war against landlords and liberate homes and apartment buildings for people who live in them.

We will police ourselves.

And arm ourselves against the pigs who come into our communities to wipe us out.

We are creating our own institutions which will gradually replace the dying institutions of Amerika.

Our media, the underground press, both creates and reflects our new conciousness. The Establishment press reflects the irrelevant, dying and repressive institutions with which we are at war.

The attack on our press is the attack on our right to think for ourselves. To destroy our culture they must destroy our media. And to protect our culture we must protect our press against pig harassment, obscenity busts and everything else.

The underground press is the beating heart of the community.

We will expropriate all businessmen.

All the nice products the hip businessmen have been packaging and selling are, in reality, dynamite which will blow up in their hands. Blow off all their fucking fingers. Blow the motherfuckers all to Kingdom Come.

Dig the Woodstock Music and Art Festival at White Lake, N.Y.: 450,000 freeks came to claim what was theirs, and the capitalists couldn't keep them out. Our joyous army overran the fences that were meant to separate us from our music.

And the capitalist pig didn't dare wage war to retrieve his rock profits. We instinctively shared what we had. There was no fear or selfishness. For three days we dominated the land and governed ourselves.

We set up free kitchens to fuck over the commercial food exploiter. We got close together to keep off the rain. We looked at our numbers and realized our POWER! It was a spontaneous triumph of anarchy. It inspires us to realize WE CANNOT BE DEFEATED.

After the White Lake demonstration of power, tickets are as obsolete as the Fillmore East.

We will demolish the rock palaces.

We will rip down the fences.

We will rip off the rip-off artists.

We will let our music free.

We will govern ourselves.

Al Copeland

The pigs came with gas and clubs to keep us out of the Pentagon.

The pigs came with gas and clubs to keep us from celebrating life in Czechago.

The pigs came with gas and shotguns to destroy a *People's* Park in Berkeley.

What would have happened if 450,000 would have massed in front of the Pentagon?

How about 450,000 in the streets of Czechago?

What if 450,000 went to Berkeley to liberate People's Park?

What would you do if 450,000 freeks marched into your town?

When the schools close down for good in the next few years, millions of free young people will overwhelm every city and town in Amerika.

We're on our way, motherfuckers!

Our politics is our music, our smell, our skin, our hair, our warm naked bodies, our drugs, our energy, our underground papers, our vision.

Our very existence is a threat to the international balance of power.

**WE CANNOT BE CO-OPTED
BECAUSE WE WANT EVERYTHING.**

41: We Are All Eldridge Cleaver

Amerika makes the classic mistake of all dying societies:

She underestimates her own children.

She thinks she can silence us through fear and punishment.

"YOU CAN JAIL A REVOLUTIONARY BUT YOU CANNOT JAIL THE REVOLUTION," proclaimed Bobby Seale, national chairman of the Black Panther Party, as he was jailed without bail on a frame-up "conspiracy to murder" rap, becoming the Panthers 48th political prisoner in one year.

"YOU'RE A PIG! YOU'RE A PUNK! YOU WILL DIE!" shouted White Panther John Sinclair, pointing at the undercover narc and the judge who had just sentenced him to 9½ to 10 years in jail for possession of two joints.

Magdalene Sinclair

Once upon a time we thought we could end poverty, racism and war by nonviolent sit-ins and moral pleas.

The days of innocence are over.

Four years of fighting experience have taught us bitter lessons.

We live in a land which has declared war on its own children, on the future.

We live in the midst of a dying beast that will kill anything that moves.

To be young is a crime.

Any crowd of kids automatically constitutes a riot.

The Law has become Illegal.

Our bravest brothers are beaten and killed in the streets, exiled to strange lands, or thrown into detention camps called jails.

Everything beautiful we build is smashed by pigs' clubs.

We get our education in courtrooms, not classrooms.

We are faced with two choices:

OBEY or PERISH.

We are fighting for our very survival as a generation.

Every young person has at least one personal atrocity story. Mine are about typical: two 30-day jail sentences, another on appeal, a phony dope bust, admitted federal wiretapping, an undercover cop, 24-hour-a-day police tail, travel restrictions, $25,000 bail/ransom and a federal conspiracy-to-riot indictment.

A young person without an arrest record has been living his life in a closet.

Their goal is to tie our hands with legal self-defense so that we have no time for revolution, and to make *some of us* an example in order to frighten and silence *you.*

The purpose of undercover cops is to make us distrustful of every new person we meet. The purpose of wire-tapping is to make us afraid to talk to each other on the phone.

They try to teach us cynicism, because cynicism is death to the revolutionary spirit.

The goal of repression is to smash and destroy the trust, optimism and spontaneity that inspires us to revolution.

Fuck 'em.

I hope they have a special Jerry Rubin Department in the CIA, staffed with bureaucrats, files, computers, psychiatrists, pharmacologists, palm-readers, astrologists, soothsayers and maybe a general or two.

We know Amerika is a paper tiger. Barefoot Viet Kong are kicking the shit out of her. Tiny Cuba, just 90 miles off Amerika's shores, broke away from the empire.

Every Cuban and every Vietnamese, *to the last man*, is ready to kill and die for their country's freedom. No oppressor can defeat a united people.

Barbed-wire fences, pig-clubs, tear gas and political arrests are the dying spasms of a government that has lost the support of the people whose lives it tries to run.

By attacking us, the Man brings us *together*.

We find that we have only Each Other. We discover ourselves capable of impulsive heroic actions.

We discover the love and brotherhood of a community that is fighting together for its own survival.

Amerika is falling apart: the alternative is revolution or catastrophe.

The revolution has replaced the church as the country's moral authority.

The revolution has replaced the economy as the way of self-expression among kids.

243

The revolution has replaced the schools as the country's educational institution.

The middle-class pleads with us: stop. Stop. STOP! "You will bring fascism down on all of us."

They sympathize with us. "Hope you don't go to jail, Jerry." "Let me know what I can do."

Fuck sympathy.

We need brothers, not mothers.

The respectable middle class must begin wholesale and collective civil disobedience to clog the courtrooms and the jails.

If we are united, we cannot be defeated. As Eldridge said, "There are more people than pigs."

We freeks must develop whatever weapons we need to survive as a generation.

If they throw tear gas at us, we'll throw it back.

If they shoot at us, we'll shoot back.

Guns.

Karate.

Explosives.

LSD in the water supply.

Togetherness.

Collectives.

Love.

Would the pigs have dared to invade People's Park if the Berkeley brothers and sisters were all armed and ready to kill and be killed?

What if 1,000 persons show up at the next trial to answer to the name of Eldridge Cleaver, John Sinclair or Dave Dellinger?

"I am Eldridge Cleaver."

"No, I am Eldridge Cleaver."

"No, I am Eldridge Cleaver."

Everyone stands with clenched fist and screams: "I
AM ELDRIDGE CLEAVER."
We Are All Eldridge Cleaver.
An attack on *any one of us* is an attack *on all of us*.
WE ARE ALL ONE!

42: The Viet Kong Are Everywhere

There is no such thing as an antiwar movement. That is a concept created by the mass media to fuck up our minds. What's happening is energy exploding in thousands of directions and people declaring themselves free.

Free from property hang-ups, free from success fixations, free from positions, titles, names, hierarchies, responsibilities, schedules, rules, routines, regular habits.

I'm not interested in the so-called antiwar movement —I'm interested in Detroit, Newark, campus disruptions, everyone smoking pot, people learning to speak out and be different.

The capitalist—money—bureaucratic—imperialist— middle-class—boring—exploitative—military—world-structure is crumbling.

The world laughs at Amerika's clumsy, bully attempt to defeat peasant warriors called Viet Kong in a never-never land called Vietnam.

And in Amerika we are all learning how to become Viet Kong.

*   *   *

If there was one lesson learned at the Pentagon and at Czechago it is that the young people didn't give a fuck about the political theories, ideologies, plans, organizations, meetings or negotiations with the cops.

The activists came to act out of their own sense of what was real.

The only vanguard is the vanguard in action.

All those hundreds of hours of bullshit meetings were just that—bullshit—better we should have spent the time listening to the Stones.

An antiwar movement is self-defeating and a waste of time because it is negative. People want to be for, not against. We don't need an antiwar movement; we need an Amerikan Liberation Movement.

Amerika is trapped within her own contradictions, and it's a joy to watch Huntley-Brinkley and see Amerika squirm. The products of Amerika are not interested in inheriting and protecting a world made for them. We are interested in creating a new world.

The Vietnam war is an old man's war; old men are trying to impose old ideas like property, racism, military force—big countries controlling little countries—upon the new world that is bursting forth in this century.

Ah, that new world!

The people looting in Detroit.

The teenagers who spit at the Pentagon and redecorated it with urine, and slogans like: "Che Lives."

The guerrillas carrying Che's actions throughout Latin America, Asia, Africa.

The thousands of young people in Amerika beginning to ask "why" and finding out that their elders have no answers; they have only power and age.

That's not an "antiwar movement"—those are movements for liberation, for freedom.

*　　*　　*

All these movements for liberation add up to a massive energy force which weakens the ability of the U.S. to carry out the war and all her other decrepit policies.

I support everything which puts people into motion, which creates a disruption and controversy, which creates chaos and rebirth.

Adlai Stevenson made me a radical in 1952 by picking up my hopes for change. The system crushed those hopes.

Eugene McCarthy has trained the street demonstrators of tomorrow in the futility of party politics.

The revolution is taking place everywhere.

The stable middle-class home is falling apart.

The church cannot attract its own children.

The schools are becoming centers of rebellion, and the streets are theaters of political action.

I approve of letters to the editor, peace candidates and peace referendums, marches, symbolic sit-ins, disruptive sit-ins, disruptive street demonstrations and sabotage.

That is guerrilla war in Amerika: everyone doing his own thing, a symphony of varied styles, rebellion for every member of the family, each to his own alienation.

The respectable middle class debates Nixon while we try to pull down his pants.

A good question: Can Amerika be changed through "peaceful transition"?

Can the beast be tamed within her own rules and regulations? Within the electoral system, within law and order, within police permits and regulations, within the boundaries of middle-class Amerika?

Can a society which makes distinctions between rich and poor, white and black, employers and employees, landlords and tenants, teachers and students, reform itself? Is it interested in reform, or just interested in eliminating nuisance? What's needed is a new generation of nuisances.

A new generation of people who are freaky, crazy, irrational, sexy, angry, irreligious, childish and mad.

people who burn draft cards and dollar bills

people who burn MA and doctoral degrees

people who say: "To hell with your goals"

people who lure the youth with music, pot and LSD

people who proudly carry Viet Kong flags

people who redefine reality, who redefine the norm

people who wear funny costumes

people who see property as theft

people who say "fuck" on television

people who break with the status-role-title-consumer game

people who have nothing material to lose but their bodies

The war in Vietnam will be stopped by the United States when the embarrassment of carrying on the war becomes greater than the embarrassment of admitting defeat.

A lot of things embarrass Amerika, a lot of things embarrass a country so dependent on images.

Youth alienation, campus demonstrations and disruptions, peace candidates, Underground Railroads of draft dodgers to Canada, trips to banned countries, thousands of people giving the middle finger to the Pentagon over national television.

We can end this war—we've got Amerika on the run. We've combined youth, music, sex, drugs and rebellion with treason—and that's a combination hard to beat.

*   *   *

What the Socialist Workers and the Communist Party, with their conversions of Marxism into a natural science, fail to understand is that language does not radicalize people—what changes people is the emotional involvement of action.

What breaks through apathy and complacency are confrontations and actions, the creation of new situations which previous mental pictures do not explain, polarizations which define people into rapidly new situations.

The struggle against the war is freeing Amerikan youth from authority hang-ups and teaching us democracy through action.

249

Every draft-card burning is a body blow to Mother Amerika because its impact sweeps throughout the elementary schools with the message: baby, something's happening, and your teachers don't know what it is, and the draft is not sacred or from heaven, or from Washington or Jefferson, it is up to you.

The movement is a school and its teachers are the Fugs/Dylan/Beatles/Ginsberg/mass media/hippies/students fighting cops in Berkeley/blood on draft records/sit-ins/jail.

Repression turns demonstration/protests into wars; actors into heroes; masses of individuals into a community; repression eliminates the bystander, the neutral observer, the theorist; it forces everyone to pick a side.

A movement cannot grow without repression.

The left needs an attack from the center and the right.

Life is theater and we are the guerrillas attacking the shrines of authority, from the priest, to the holy dollar, to the two-party system, zapping people's minds and putting them through changes in actions in which everyone is emotionally involved.

The street is the stage.

You are the star of the show and everything you were once taught is up for grabs.

The longhaired beast smoking pot, evading the draft and stopping traffic during demonstrations is a hell of a bigger threat to the system than the so-called "politicos" with their leaflets of support for the Viet Kong and the coming working-class revolution. Politics is how you live your life, not whom you vote for.

*   *   *

The most important political conflict in the United States today is the generational conflict.

We are all under the influence of a collective historical unconscious.

Communism to us means not Stalin, but the heroic romantic Fidel/Che/Viet Kong.

Hitler to us represents words on paper.

We are optimistic and idealistic about the future. Our 1984 will be great.

The economy is rich; overproduction is the problem; now everyone can dig life, and we know it. Life can be a trip.

We want a communal world where the imagination runs supreme, and where human institutions respond to human needs. Feeling and emotion will be unsuppressed. Everything will be free. People will go to museums to look at dollar bills. There will be no nations, only rich communities and rich cultures.

This generational movement cuts across class and race lines.

The generational revolt in Amerika is not explained by Freud or Marx. It is a war between historical generations, and the future belongs to us because Amerika is defending institutions and ideas like ownership and nation—and these institutions no longer respond to needs.

We did not build CBS, the Democratic Party or the Catholic Church, and we want no place in them.

Vietnam is a case of the past trying to suppress the future.

The Amerikan economy has rendered white middle-class youth and black working-class youth useless, because we are not needed to make the economy run. Uselessness breeds revolution. The only exciting and meaningful thing to do in Amerika today is to disrupt her institutions and build new ones.

*　　　*　　　*

Subvert!!

That's the task of every young person. Spread ideas that undercut the consistent world of Amerika, and then top it off by burning her symbols—from draft cards to flags to dollar bills.

We must alienate middle-class Amerika. We must get middle-class Amerika all whipped up emotionally.

Amerika suffers from a great cancer; it's called APATHY.

Moral persuasion may work on the guilt feelings of the Amerikan middle class; it may even win his mind or vote; but how are you going to get him off his ass?

Alienating people is a necessary process in getting them to move.

Mr. Amerika: The War is at Home.

It is not on Huntley-Brinkley; it is right outside your window; wait, now it's inside your living room in your kid's head.

When we were simply marching and petitioning and making moral pleas to the government to end the war, the good hard common sense soul of Amerika knew we were only kids, that we were not serious.

Amerikans know how hard it is to move City Hall.

"Ah, c'mon off it, you ain't going to end the war that way" was the truck driver's likely response to vigils, marches, peace candidates and peace literature.

Instinctively, the Amerikan knew more about his government than did the "antiwar movement."

He knew that it was way up there, made up of good-for-nothing politicians, hard to reach and then reachable only through the language of power and violence.

When the movement moved into the streets, and began to act in the dialect of power, when the movement got tough, we broke away all those barriers preventing us from reaching the average guy. Amerika understands Eldridge Cleaver and Amerika understands peace demonstrators fighting in the streets, and that's why we are much more dangerous than a hundred Martin Luther Kings.

Disruption of Amerikan society is becoming about as frequent as Yankee planes over Vietnam.

Persuasion follows the disruption.

Crisis replaces the coffee break.

43 : Scenario for the Future/Yippieland

Every high school and college in the country will close with riots and sabotage and cops will circle the campuses, standing shoulder to shoulder. The schools belong to the pigs.

Millions of young people will surge into the streets of every city, dancing, singing, smoking pot, fucking in the streets, tripping, burning draft cards, stopping traffic.

The Pentagon will send troops to fight spreading guerrilla wars in Laos, Thailand, Indonesia, India, the Congo, Bolivia, South Africa, Brazil, France.

High government officials will defect to the yippies.

The State Department will discover its highest ranks infested with the yippie symps. Black cops will join the black-and-white liberation army in the streets.

High school students will seize radio, TV and newspaper offices across the land.

Police stations will blow up.

Revolutionaries will break into jails and free all the prisoners.

Clerical workers will ax their computers and put chewing gum into the machines.

Army platoons and the National Guard will desert to the revolution, bringing their guns with them.

Workers will seize their factories and begin running them communally, without profit.

Shorthairs will become longhairs overnight.

Yippie helicopter pilots will bomb police positions with LSD-gas.

The Pentagon will strafe yippie bases, and we'll shoot the planes out of the sky.

Kids will lock their parents out of their suburban homes and turn them into guerrilla bases, storing arms.

We'll break into banks and join the bank tellers in taking all the money and burning it in gigantic bonfires in the middle of the city.

Previous revolutions aimed at seizure of the state's highest authority, followed by the takeover of the means of production. The Youth International Revolution will begin with mass breakdown of authority, mass rebellion, total anarchy in every institution in the Western world. Tribes of longhairs, blacks, armed women, workers, peasants and students will take over.

The yippie dropout myth will infiltrate every structure of Amerika. The revolution will shock itself by discovering that it has friends everywhere, friends just waiting for The Moment.

At community meetings all over the land, Bob Dylan will replace The National Anthem.

There will be no more jails, courts or police.

The White House will become a crash pad for anybody without a place to stay in Washington.

The world will become one big commune with free food and housing, everything shared.

All watches and clocks will be destroyed.

Barbers will go to rehabilitation camps where they will grow their hair long.

There will be no such crime as "stealing" because everything will be free.

The Pentagon will be replaced by an LSD experimental farm.

There will be no more schools or churches because the entire world will become one church and school.

People will farm in the morning, make music in the afternoon and fuck wherever and whenever they want to.

The United States of Amerika will become a tiny yippie island in a vast sea of Yippieland love.